EX LIBRIS

VINTAGE **CLASSICS**

ONO NO KOMACHI

Ono no Komachi was a legendary figure from the time of her death. Little is known about her life, but historians believe Komachi served the Heian court in the middle of the ninth century. She most likely had at least one child. The legend goes that she was not only the outstanding poet of her time, but the most beautiful, though the story told in Noh theatre is that she ended her days in poverty and obscurity.

IZUMI SHIKIBU

Izumi Shikibu, born *c.* 974, was the daughter of a lord. She arrived at the Heian court to serve a former empress. During her time there she had two prominent love affairs with men who both died, was embroiled in scandal, and was married and divorced. On marrying her second husband she accompanied him to his post in the provinces and never returned to court life. She is thought to have died around the age of sixty. Her reputation as a poet grew after her death and she is now regarded as one of the outstanding poets of Japanese literature.

JANE HIRSHFIELD

Jane Hirshfield, recipient of a Guggenheim Fellowship and other awards for her poetry, is the author of many books, including *Of Gravity & Angels* and *Alaya*. Her work has appeared in the *New Yorker*, the *Atlantic*, the *Paris Review* and elsewhere. She lives in Mill Valley, California.

MARIKO ARATANI

Mariko Aratani is a graduate of Tokyo National University of Fine Arts and Music. A musician, weaver and translator, she currently lives in San Francisco.

ONO NO KOMACHI & IZUMI SHIKIBU

The Ink Dark Moon

TRANSLATED BY

Jane Hirshfield

WITH

Mariko Aratani

WITH A FOREWORD BY

Nikita Gill

VINTAGE

3 5 7 9 10 8 6 4

Vintage Classics is part of the Penguin Random House group of companies
whose addresses can be found at global.penguinrandomhouse.com

This edition published in Vintage Classics in 2023
First published in the United States of America by Vintage Classics in 1986

Poems from this book have previously appeared in *The American Poetry Review*,
Ironwood, *Northcoast View* and *Yellow Silk*.

penguin.co.uk/vintage-classics

Typeset in 10.75/13.25pt Perpetua MT Pro by Jouve (UK), Milton Keynes
Printed and bound in Great Britain by Clays Ltd, Elcograf S.p.A.

The authorised representative in the EEA is Penguin Random House Ireland,
Morrison Chambers, 32 Nassau Street, Dublin D02 YH68

A CIP catalogue record for this book is available from the British Library

ISBN 9781784878245

Penguin Random House is committed to a sustainable future
for our business, our readers and our planet. This book is made
from Forest Stewardship Council® certified paper.

TRANSLATORS' ACKNOWLEDGMENTS

We would like to thank Lily Pond, editor of *Yellow Silk*, who introduced us and published the first fruits of this project; Michael Katz, our agent and unofficial third partner; Charles Levine, for his early support and encouragement; Kaz Tanahashi, for his generosity in reviewing the appendix; and Luann Walther, our Vintage editor. Jane Hirshfield would also like to thank Karen Brazell, whose courses introduced her to the poets translated here, and the John Simon Guggenheim Memorial Foundation, for their support of her work during the year this project was begun.

CONTENTS

FOREWORD

A long time ago, my great-grandmother told me that poetry was the language of love, of both the joyful and the broken heart. She told me over a cup of tea on a misty morning that poems are where love can exist in its truest form. Poems never judge love for being too passionate, too despondent or too wistful. In fact, poems say 'give in' to the intensity and let your feelings dance across the page. I think this is why, across countless cultures and languages, the love poem remains evergreen, an immortal jewel untouched by the weathering of time.

My great-grandmother was a poet. She is the only poet in my entire family other than myself. She was never published. I only know of her poetry because of a small, ornately carved mahogany wooden box, in which there were scores of pages. Pages full of love poems with an intensity and honesty that prose resists. My great-grandmother kept them bound in a crimson ribbon, the box always smelling of fresh lavender from the garden. The paper had yellowed with time, but when she read them, you could see in the glow of her smile that she was transported to another place, another time in her life when that love was fresh and new. She had a collection of old love poetry books she returned to often – a golden warmth in her voice when she read some of them aloud. I was only a child then, but what better example could you possibly have than seeing the magic of love poems in someone's life.

The poems in this book remind me of that early revelation – my first experience with the power of love poetry. Although written in the ninth and tenth centuries, the words here speak powerfully to me, illustrating without a doubt that poetry is the language of love, and like love, stands the test of time. I often say that poetry is an ancient artform that is in the habit of reinventing itself in the hands and minds of the poets of any era. What I have learned after reading *The Ink Dark Moon* is that some poems stand the test of time and give something new to each new generation that reads them.

My great-grandmother once said that she wrote poems because it was an act of courage and hope to put pen to paper and write vulnerably. Ceaselessly, these poems say that love is courage and hope, but also longing and loss. That where grief exists, so does life, and that beauty can be found in the heart of tragedy. They speak with a yearning and passion that everyone who has ever been in love can recognise. This is the very same vulnerability my great-grandmother so deeply treasured.

This vulnerability is clear from the very first page, where Ono no Komachi takes us into the dreamscapes of longing, her poems capturing the restlessness of unrequited love. My great-grandmother once told me that the tragedy of loving someone who does not love you back, or who cannot love, is as painful a condition as the heart can endure while still beating; these poems capture this with devastating brevity. Anyone who has ever been through such an ache will identify with the words:

Night deepens
with the sound
of a calling deer,
and I hear
my own one-sided love.

But not all of it is about ache, as not all of love is about tragedy. So much of love holds joy. A gentle playfulness lives in Ono no Komachi's poems which made me smile: there is a poem here about morning glories and another about the flower of forgetting that I recommend everyone reads to truly experience her wondrous wit.

I think humour in poetry – the capacity to make the reader smile or even laugh – is a difficult art to master. Too much and the levity can take away from the poem; too little and it escapes the reader. These poems are able to master humour with precision in just thirty-one syllables without losing the weight of the verse.

The tanka form looks deceptively simple. It is not, and not only because it adheres to a tight format. Every syllable counts and to draw rich images, rhythm and meaning, all within thirty-one syllables, is a hard job for even the more proficient of poets. The translators show Ono no Komachi and Izumi Shikibu crafting it effortlessly.

Where Ono no Komachi's poems blend the playful with longing, Izumi Shikibu's work brings the complexity and devastation of grief after losing a good love. There is a specific kind of haunting in her poems – a feeling that sometimes you can sense the ghost of a love long gone within the verses. A poem that I think of often when remembering love lost is this:

> Why haven't I
> thought of it before?
> This body,
> remembering yours,
> is the keepsake you left.

Balancing out the heaviness of grief in these poems is a series of sprightly response poems that reveal a lively, sharp intellect. I found myself chuckling at one in particular which was sent to (presumably) a lover who had left their purple robe behind! The boldness here is reflective of a more modern poetry, a poetry I have seen performed on stages and on social media.

Such is the timeless nature of both Ono no Komachi and Izumi Shikibu's writings that one almost forgets that these poems were written in the ninth and tenth centuries during Japan's Heian era. On first reading, I read aloud a few of their poems to friends who were awed by how perfectly they capture modern love. I often share poems with friends who do not read poetry, and the fact that so many of them responded well is a testament to the authenticity and warmth of these poems. This is important to someone like me who has always valued accessible language. The verse is inviting rather than insular, while holding the integrity of the interior world of the poet.

The work also proves that brevity does not come at the expense of imagery or musicality. It negates the idea that short-form poetry lacks in any way in comparison to long-form poetry where the poet has more space to play. The rich imagery of autumn and foxfire, flowers and dawns, and even the cadence of a river flowing are captured vividly, and I am repeatedly drawn back to the stunning turns of poetics which adhere so firmly to structure.

At the heart of this collection are women who are passionately and deeply in love with life as much as they are with the lovers they speak of through these pages. They have a razor-sharp wit and a keen sense of radical observation, rebuking any stereotype of submissiveness placed upon women from antiquity. Ono no Komachi and Izumi Shikibu were celebrated in their time and their work is legendary for good reason.

I have a great admiration for poets who can speak across generations. The kind of poets a grandmother passes down to her grandchild or the kind of poet multiple generations of a family can read because their words remain so current, enduring the test of time to reach out across history.

I wish I could have given my great-grandmother this book. It would have confirmed for her that her belief was true: love and poetry are synonymous. She would have treasured this collection, but beyond that, she would have admired the work of these legendary women who walked many hundreds of years before her. Their courage and their zest for life, even a life where grief came to visit or a lover was lost forever, would have inspired her endlessly.

My great-grandmother is no longer with us but her teachings about poetry have remained with me till this day. Be vulnerable. Trust in your heart's truest voice – the language of love is simple and pure. And have the courage to put pen to paper always for the women who walked before you, and the women who will come after you. And this is precisely why she would have loved this book.

My great-grandmother never got to see her words in print. And I wonder sometimes how many of our foremothers wrote love poems and hid them away in small wooden boxes, the smell of lavender unspooling across the room whenever this box was opened. I wonder how many foremothers in poetry we have lost to the sands of time.

It is a blessing, then, to have read a book where the voices of two foremothers within poetry are so strong and the poems so breathtaking. Poems which show us so clearly that love knows its favoured language is poetry.

I am so glad this book exists.

And when you read it, you will be too.

Nikita Gill, 2023

INTRODUCTION

The two poets whose work is collected in *The Ink Dark Moon* are central figures in the only Golden Age in literary history in which women writers were the predominant geniuses: Japan's Heian era, which lasted from 794 to 1185. Ono no Komachi (834?–?) served at the imperial court in the capital city of Heian-kyo (present-day Kyoto) during the first half century of its existence; her poetry, deeply subjective, passionate, and complex, helped to usher in a poetic age of personal expressiveness, technical excellence, and philosophical and emotional depth. Izumi Shikibu (974?–1034?) wrote during the time of the court culture's greatest flowering; a woman committed to a life of both religious consciousness and erotic intensity, Shikibu explored her experience in language that is precise in observation, intimate, lyrical, and deeply moving. These two women, the first a pivotal figure who became legendary in Japanese literary history, the second Japan's major woman poet, illuminated certain areas of human experience with a beauty, truthfulness, and compression unsurpassed in the literature of any other age. As do the words of Sappho, Catullus, and Dickinson, in whose company they belong, their brief poems serve as small but utterly clear windows into those concerns of heart and mind that persist unchanged from culture to culture and from millennium to millennium.

*

The aristocratic culture of the Heian court proved to be a uniquely auspicious environment for women writers for several reasons, but the foremost is the central role of the arts in the conduct of daily life. Aside from the unalterable circumstance of inherited family rank, successful display of aesthetic sensibility was the primary means of establishing personal distinction among members of the court, both male and female. The skills, subtle judgment, and taste demonstrated in the mixing of incense, the layering of patterned silk kimonos, musical performance, painting, dance, and above all the writing and recitation of poetry, figured greatly both in one's appeal as a prospective romantic partner and in one's prospects for official advancement. No significant experience was considered complete without its accompanying poem, and conversely, the desire to give an experience formal expression in poetry was itself the mark of the presence of deep emotion for an educated person.

Male writers, however, composed a great part of their work in Chinese; adopted in the fourth or fifth century as Japan's first written language, Chinese served as the official form of communication in government and scholarly discourse in much the way that Latin functioned in European courts and centers of learning in the Middle Ages. Women, who were not usually educated in the use of Chinese, were only given the means for creating a written literature near the end of the eighth century, when a new system was devised for using Chinese characters phonetically to transcribe spoken Japanese. Concentrating their efforts on the vernacular, and free from male writers' need to satisfy the requirements of foreign poetic structures and sensibilities, women could devote themselves to developing their literary potential to the highest degree in the poems, diaries, and "tales" in which they recorded both the public and the most private and deeply felt aspects of their lives.

*

A few themes dominate the poetry of the Heian period (and that of later periods as well); each of them is touched on in the opening sentences of the most famous critical statement of Japanese literature, Ki no Tsurayuki's preface to the *Kokinshū* (*c.* 905), the first of a series of imperial anthologies in which the best works in Japanese of poets "ancient and modern" were collected:

> The poetry of Japan has its seeds in the human heart and mind and grows into the myriad leaves of words. Because people experience many different phenomena in this world, they express that which they think and feel in their hearts in terms of all that they see and hear. A nightingale singing among the blossoms, the voice of a pond-dwelling frog—listening to these, what living being would not respond with his own poem? It is poetry which effortlessly moves the heavens and the earth, awakens the world of invisible spirits to deep feeling, softens the relationship between men and women, and consoles the hearts of fierce warriors.

Here named as poetry's proper concerns are human emotion in general; thoughts raised by observing the sights and sounds of the natural world; religion; the taming of wildness of spirit; and, central to much of the work in this collection, the relations between men and women. Poetry is described as the natural upwelling of language in an awakened and interested heart—an irresistible and effortless answering within the individual to the continual calling of the Other, whether natural, supernatural, or human—and as possessing a virtually magical power to change and ameliorate the external order of life. What is extraordinary about the place of poetry in Heian Japan is that this conception of its fundamental importance was not confined to a select few known as "writers" but shared by all members of the court society, for whom every personal or ceremonial experience, whether public or private, called for not only the composing of a verse but also the recollection of earlier poems which might add their resonance to the moment. The first opening of the spring blossoms, the death of a child, a glimpse of the moon, an official ritual, even the return of a forgotten fan—none was complete without an accompanying poem. And, for the purpose of "softening the relations between men and women," poetry was ubiquitous.

One thousand years ago Heian-kyo was more populous than any European city, one of very few centers of high civilization anywhere in the world. Male members of the aristocracy vied for political favor and positions of power; daughters of aristocratic families were sent at about age fourteen to serve as companions to members of the imperial household. Because it was solely by a daughter's marriage that a family's status might be permanently advanced, the women serving in the imperial retinue were highly cultured and carefully educated, and they were considered aesthetic equals by the men. Once ensconced in their separate living quarters, the women had a few official duties, but for the most part they were left to their own devices. They read and exchanged copies of anthologies, prepared themselves with the help of their maids for the excitement of outings, played musical instruments or wrote for their own and each other's entertainment, and generally kept one another and the empress they served amused. But the greatest part of their attention, it seems, was devoted to affairs of the heart: love affairs were an accepted part of courtship for unmarried women, and polygamy was the usual arrangement for men. Thus, erotic love and its consequences were perennial conversational and literary topics.

For a high-ranking member of the Heian court, relations with the opposite sex presented a larger range of possible outcomes and a greater flexibility than in most cultures. Although a primary marriage at an early age was often arranged by the family, a man could take as many secondary wives or official mistresses as he wished, and as many secret lovers as would accommodate him. A man might install a number of secondary wives in his home—most Heian dwellings contained several wings or compounds—or he could have several wives living in different locations. An unmarried woman might also have multiple lovers, if perhaps with greater discretion; a wife, by contrast, was confined to a single husband and was expected to remain faithful after marriage, although, as can be seen in the life of Izumi Shikibu, this was not always the case. Despite this mild double standard, Heian women were accorded a great deal of independence in romantic matters: able to own property and receive income in her own name, a woman could refuse a suitor's advances, or, should a marriage or her position as an official "second wife" no longer suit her, end a relationship entirely through divorce or by moving away. Furthermore, since nearly all encounters between members of the opposite sexes took place within a convention of secrecy, the opinions of family or friends about one's choices in the realm of eros might be avoided for quite a long time.

The first intimation of a new romance for a woman of the court was the arrival at her door of a messenger bearing a five-line poem in an unfamiliar hand. If the woman found the poem sufficiently intriguing, the paper it was written on suitable for its contents and mood, and the calligraphy acceptably graceful, her encouraging reply—itself in the form of a poem—would set in motion a clandestine, late-night visit from her suitor. The first night together was, according to established etiquette, sleepless; lovemaking and talk were expected to continue without pause until the man, protesting the night's brevity, departed in the first light of the predawn. Even then he was not free to turn his thoughts to the day's official duties: a morning-after poem had to be written and sent off by means of an ever-present messenger page, who would return with the woman's reply. Only after this exchange had been completed could the night's success be fully judged by whether the poems were equally ardent and accomplished, referring in image and nuance to the themes of the night just passed. Subsequent visits were made on the same clandestine basis and under the same circumstances, until the relationship was either made official by a private ceremony of marriage or ended.

Once she had given her heart, a woman was left to await her lover's letters and appearances at her door at nightfall. Should he fail to arrive, there might be many explanations—the darkness of the night, inclement weather, inauspicious omens preventing travel, or other interests. Many sleepless nights were spent in hope and speculation, and, as evidenced by the poems in this book, in poetic activity. Throughout the course of a relationship, the exchange of poems served to reassure, remind, rekindle or cool interest, and, in general, to keep the other person aware of a lover's state of mind. At the same time, poetry was a means of expressing solely for oneself the uncertainties, hopes, and doubts which inevitably accompanied such a system of courtship, as well as a way of exploring other personal concerns.

With so many striving to bring art to everyday communication, the few who truly excelled acquired extraordinary prestige and charisma. Ono no Komachi, in particular, became the subject of legend almost from the time of her death. Little is known about her life, and the stories about her freely commingle historic fact and suppositions drawn from the poems. Historians believe Komachi to have been the daughter of the lord of Dewa and to have served the court in the middle of the ninth century; she probably had at least one child, as a poem in a later imperial anthology is attributed to "Komachi's grandchild." Legends, folktales, and songs add that Komachi was not only the outstanding woman poet of her time but also the most beautiful and desirable of women. (In the culture of the Heian court, the ability to write poems of great beauty would in itself have been a major cause for being thought both personally attractive and desirable.) Also according to legend, the renowned poet ended her life in anonymity, isolation, and poverty, an ancient, half-mad hag living outside the city walls, though still writing poetry and possessing a deep understanding of Buddhist teachings.

One version of Komachi's final years appears in *Komachi at Sekidera*, thought to be the greatest Nō play, which was written 500 years after her death. In the play a Buddhist priest takes his young poetry students into the countryside to visit a hundred-year-old woman who is believed to know the secrets of the art of poetry. During their conversation the crone in her straw hut casually reveals that she herself is the great Komachi; the visitors are appropriately amazed. Near the end of the play, because it is the night of *Tanabata*, the festival celebrating both love and poetry, one of the pupils performs a ritual dance. When the child is finished, the onlookers are amazed and moved for a second time as the aged Komachi, her memories overpowering her sense of shame and decorum, painfully rises to her feet and takes her turn to dance. Two other Nō dramas show Komachi seeking salvation through Buddhism in her old age, hoping to atone for her cruelty to a lover in her youth. Whatever the facts of Komachi's life, we know that shortly after her death she was named by Ki no Tsurayuki, in his preface to the *Kokinshū*, one of the "Six Poetic Geniuses" included therein—the only woman so honored. Only a hundred or so of her poems survive, less than a tenth of what remains of Shikibu's work.

A good deal more has been recorded about the life of Izumi Shikibu, who came to the Heian court at the height of its greatness to serve a former empress. Born around 974, she too was the daughter of a lord.

Despite her marriage to a provincial official (the lord of Izumi Province, from whom she takes her name) and the birth of a daughter, Shikibu began a passionate liaison with the empress's stepson; the resulting scandal left her divorced and disowned by her family. Three years later, a year after her first lover had died, his brother, Prince Atsumichi, sent Shikibu an exploratory gift of orange blossoms, and thus commenced a new affair. In her famous *Diary*, a mixture of poetry and prose, Shikibu recounts the beginning of their love, through the time when Atsumichi persuaded her to move into his compound despite the unusually vigorous protestations and eventual departure of his primary wife. Five years later Atsumichi's death in an epidemic ended the central relationship of Shikibu's life.

Shikibu's behavior when—after a period of mourning in which she wrote over 240 poems to her departed lover—she returned to service in court, can be surmised from the following incident: Shikibu's sponsor and protector at court was Fujiwara no Michinaga, father of the empress she now served and the most powerful man in Japan. Lord Michinaga, seeing Shikibu's fan in the hands of one of her many lovers, took it and wrote on it the words "Fan of a Floating Woman." When Shikibu heard of this, despite her dependence on this ruthless and unpredictable destroyer of careers, she swiftly sent him a poem:

Some cross the Pass of Love,
some don't.
Unless you are the watchman there
it is not your right
to cast blame.

Izumi Shikibu and her fellow court attendants at the turn of the last millennium must surely have been the most illustrious company of women writers ever to share a set of roofs. Also serving Empress Akiko was Murasaki Shikibu (*Shikibu* is a title, not a surname), who kept court society eagerly awaiting each successive chapter of *The Tale of Genji*, earliest of the world's great novels. Meanwhile, in a rival empress's household, the famous Sei Shōnagon, in her *Pillow Book*, recorded with a brilliant and unsentimental eye the doings of the court women and their lovers. The work of many other accomplished women of this court society has come down to us as well, including poems by Izumi Shikibu's daughter, Naishi.

When she was thirty-six Shikibu married for the second time and accompanied her new husband to his post in the provinces. She never returned to court life and is thought to have died at the age of sixty. Her reputation as a poet grew steadily after her death, and Shikibu is now recognized as the outstanding woman poet of Japanese literature.

Both Shikibu and Komachi were not only deeply passionate but also intensely religious; an inquiry into the deeper questions of life runs through the core of each woman's work. We know that Izumi Shikibu departed the hot-house atmosphere of the court from time to time to stay in one of the small Buddhist mountain monasteries where guests might live among the monks for limited periods of contemplation and retreat; at one point she seriously considered becoming a nun. Similarly, Komachi's poems reflect a deeply Buddhist view of existence as ceaseless change and return again and again to the question of what in our experience can be called "real." One of the deep pleasures in reading their poetry is discovering the way that, for these women, the metaphysics of religious teaching and the tumultuous course of the heart in love confirm a single truth, the impermanence of being. The endeavor to come to some acceptance and understanding of this unavoidable transience profoundly illuminates their work.

Komachi and Shikibu stand out as two of the greatest poets in an age of greatness not simply because they achieved technical virtuosity in their chosen form, the thirty-one-syllable *tanka* verse, but because they used that form as a medium of reflection and introspection. Each confronted her experience with a directness and honesty unusual in any age. The result is that a thousand years later we can read poems that remain absolutely accurate and moving descriptions of our most common and central experiences: love and loss, their reflection in the loveliness and evanescence of the natural world, and the effort to understand better the nature of being. We turn to these poems not to discover the past but to experience the present more deeply. In this way they satisfy the test of all great literature, for it is our own lives we find illuminated in them.

THE INK DARK MOON

ONO NO KOMACHI

Did he appear
because I fell asleep
thinking of him?
If only I'd known I was dreaming,
I'd never have wakened.

When my desire
grows too fierce
I wear my bed clothes
inside out,
dark as the night's rough husk.

My longing for you—
too strong to keep within bounds.
At least no one can blame me
when I go to you at night
along the road of dreams.

No way to see him
on this moonless night—
I lie awake longing, burning,
breasts racing fire,
heart in flames.

After a lover visited in secrecy

I know it must be this way
in the waking world,
but how cruel—
even in my dreams
we hide from others' eyes.

Though I go to him constantly
on the paths of dream,
never resting my feet,
in the real world
it doesn't equal a single glance.

Night deepens
with the sound
of a calling deer,
and I hear
my own one-sided love.

If this were a dream
I would surely
see you again—
why must waking love
be left incomplete?

The cicadas sing
in the twilight
of my mountain village—
tonight, no one
will visit save the wind.

A diver does not abandon
a seaweed-filled bay. . . .
Will you then turn away
from this floating, sea-foam body
that waits for your gathering hands?

Awake tonight
with loneliness,
I cannot keep myself
from longing
for the handsome moon.

Is this love reality
or a dream?
I cannot know,
when both reality and dreams
exist without truly existing.

Tokiwa Mountain's
pine trees are always green—
I wonder,
do they recognize autumn
in the sound of the blowing wind?

Although there is
not one moment
without longing,
still, how strange
this autumn twilight is.

This entangling wind
is just like
last autumn's gusts.
Only the dew of tears
on my sleeve is new.

Sent anonymously to a man who had passed in front of the screens of my room

Should the world of love
end in darkness,
without our glimpsing
that cloud-gap
where the moon's light fills the sky?

The autumn night
is long only in name—
We've done no more
than gaze at each other
and it's already dawn.

This morning
even my morning glories
are hiding,
not wanting to show
their sleep-mussed hair.

This inn
on the road to Iwanoue
is a cold place to sleep . . .
O monk,
would you please lend me your robes?

The monk's reply:

Those who have given up the world
wear only a single layer
of moss-rough cloth,
yet not to offer it would be heartless.
Let us sleep together, then.

I thought to pick
the flower of forgetting
for myself,
but I found it
already growing in his heart.

Sent to a man who seemed to have changed his mind

Since my heart placed me
on board your drifting ship,
not one day has passed
that I haven't been drenched
in cold waves.

The seaweed gatherer's weary feet
keep coming back to my shore.
Doesn't he know
there's no harvest for him
in this uncaring bay?

Like a ripple
that chases the slightest caress
of the breeze—
is that how you want me
to follow you?

What blossoms
yet has no fruit
is the white wave of the reef
putting on
the sea god's head.

I thought those white clouds
were gathered around
some distant peak,
but already
they have risen between us.

How sad,
to think I will end
as only
a pale green mist
drifting the far fields.

Silent as spring rain
on a marsh,
my tears
fall to my sleeves
unheard by him.

Those gifts you left
have become my enemies:
without them
there might have been
a moment's forgetting.

Since this body
was forgotten
by the one who promised to come,
my only thought is wondering
whether it even exists.

It seems a time has come
when you've become like those horses
wild with spring
who long for distant fields
where the light mists rise.

As pitiful as a diver
far out in Suma Bay
who has lost an oar from her boat,
this body
with no one to turn to.

Seeing the moonlight
spilling down
through these trees,
my heart fills to the brim
with autumn.

O Spider Lily
that grows on the mountain
called Waiting,
is there someone you also
promised to meet this autumn?

Sent in a letter attached to a rice stalk with an empty seed husk

How sad that I hope
to see you even now,
after my life has emptied itself
like this stalk of grain
into the autumn wind.

To a man who seems to have forgotten

Truly now I've grown old
in the winter rains.
Even your words of love
have altered,
falling leaves.

Yes, a mountain village
can be lonely . . .
yet living here is easier
than dwelling amid
the worries of the world.

If, in an autumn field,
a hundred flowers
can untie their streamers,
may I not also openly frolic,
as fearless of blame?

This pine tree by the rock
must have its memories too:
after a thousand years,
see how its branches
lean towards the ground.

The hunting lanterns
on Mount Ogura have gone,
the deer are calling for their mates. . . .
How easily I might sleep,
if only I didn't share their fears.

When Fun'ya no Yasuhide was appointed governor of Mikawa, he wrote asking if I would like to come visit his district. I replied:

This body
grown fragile, floating,
a reed cut from its roots. . . .
If a stream would ask me
to follow, I'd go, I think.

While watching
the long rains falling on this world
my heart, too, fades
with the unseen color
of the spring flowers.

How invisibly
it changes color
in this world,
the flower
of the human heart.

In this world
the living grow fewer,
the dead increase—
how much longer must I
carry this body of grief?

This abandoned house
shining
in the mountain village—
how many nights
has the autumn moon spent here?

IZUMI SHIKIBU

Lying alone,
my black hair tangled,
uncombed,
I long for the one
who touched it first.

Why haven't I
thought of it before?
This body,
remembering yours,
is the keepsake you left.

In this world
love has no color—
yet how deeply
my body
is stained by yours.

Wakened by the scent
of flowering plum. . . .
The darkness
of the spring night
fills me with longing.

No different, really—
a summer moth's
visible burning
and this body,
transformed by love.

A man came secretly and left in heavy rain. In the poem he sent the next morning, he mentioned having gotten wet. I replied:

Love-soaked, rain-soaked—
if people ask
which drenched
your sleeves,
what will you say?

To a man who said we should meet, even if it were only for a single time

Even if I now saw you
only once,
I would long for you
through worlds,
worlds.

Sent when returning a purple robe that a certain person had left behind

Don't blush!
People will guess
that we slept
beneath the folds
of this purple-root rubbed cloth.

In October, a man came and then left

How easily,
leaving my house,
he cuts through
the embroidered fabric
of the fall leaves!

I break off
a spray of rock azalea
to hold: in its flowers
I can see again
the red-dyed robes my husband wore.

A friend tells me the cherry trees have come into bloom

However wildly
this year's cherry blossoms bloom,
I'll see them
with the plum's scent
filling my heart.

No bone-chilling
autumn wind
could pierce me
like this spring storm
scattering blossoms.

Time passes,
a man forgets
and no longer comes;
yet still
I depend on his promises.

The fleeting world
of white dew,
fox fires, dreams—
all last long,
compared with love.

Returning home near dawn after a night away

I used to say,
"How poetic,"
but now I know
this dawn-rising men do
is merely tiresome!

A man used to come during the summer, but stopped

You no longer
come to visit me
in your splendid summer clothes—
how transparently thin
your heart is as well!

A monk came to visit and left his fan; I returned it to him with this poem:

I think
you may have briefly forgotten
this fan,
but everyone must know
how it came to be dropped!

A lover wrote to ask if he had left his obi behind. When I found it, I noticed a rip. After repairing it, I returned it with this poem:

A torn sash
can be mended.
But what if you and I
are as pulled apart
as this belt?

To someone who came from the countryside in autumn

Though we knew each other
without overlapping
our clothes,
still, with this autumn wind's sound,
I find myself waiting for you.

A pond hides herself uselessly
deep in the marsh: the horses foraging
for new growth in spring
pull the reeds
until not a single root is left.

Seeing someone holding my fan, the courtier Michinaga asked whose it was; when he heard it was mine, he took it and wrote on it the words "Fan of a Floating Woman." My response:

Some cross the Pass of Love,
some don't.
Unless you are the watchman there
it is not your right
to cast blame.

A lover accused me of unfaithfulness. At the time I said nothing, but the next morning I sent this poem:

The reason I cried?
That my tears
might become a stream
in which to rinse
this muddied name.

Written for a current wife to send to an angry ex-wife, attached to a bamboo shoot

The bamboo's
old root
hasn't changed at all—
Is there even one night
he sleeps at home? No.

If only his horse
had been tamed
by my hand—
I'd have taught it
not to follow anyone else!

To a man who wrote requesting an answer

I think I will not go out again
on your drifting boat
that floats
in any direction
without ever setting a course.

{Two Tanabata* Poems}

Don't look up
by yourself
at the sky where stars meet—
the wind from the Milky Way
blows cold.

How I envy the Tanabata Stars
their once-yearly lovemaking tonight—
in this world,
there is a woman
who doesn't know what love's future may be.

**Tanabata Festival, which takes place on the seventh night of the seventh month, celebrates lovers' meetings and poetry. On that night a gathering of magpies is said to form with their wings a bridge across the river of the heavens so that two stars can meet. The two—Altair and Vega—were once lovers, Cow Herder Boy and Weaver Girl, but were turned into stars and separated after their love caused them to neglect their duties.*

Undisturbed,
my garden fills
with summer growth—
how I wish for one
who would push the deep grass aside.

Under the water,
what is the grebe's heart like?
Seen the usual way,
from above,
how unfeeling it seems.

Summer night,
a rap at the gate,
a rap at the door . . .
how hope answers
the water rail's knock.

On a night
when the moon
shines as brightly as this,
the unspoken thoughts
of even the most discreet heart might be seen.

My pillow
has become
a dusty thing—
for whom
should I brush it off?

How to remove
this Chinese robe?
Though I cut and cut
at its fabric,
still I wear my gossip-muddied name.

Things I Want Decided

Which shouldn't exist
in this world,
the one who forgets
or the one
who is forgotten?

Which is better,
to love
one who has died
or not to see
each other when you're alive?

Which is better,
the distant lover
you long for
or the one you see daily
without desire?

Which is the least unreliable
among fickle things—
the swift rapids,
a flowing river,
or this human world?

From every branch
flowers drift and mingle down.
Saying "Now!"
the spring departs until the paths
she takes in leaving cannot be seen.

I cannot say
which is which:
the glowing
plum blossom *is*
the spring night's moon.

The world rushes on
and now spring is over.
It seems that only yesterday
everything I saw
was in full flower.

Although
the cricket's song
has no words,
still,
it sounds like sorrow.

Tonight,
with no one to wait for,
why do my thoughts
deepen
along with the twilight?

At a time when I had just gone into mourning a friend wrote to ask if I had noticed how bright the moon was the night before. I replied:

Even your kind words
only cause sorrow—
the moonlight
doesn't stop
on an ink-dyed sleeve.

Last year's
fragile, vanished snow
is falling now again—
if only seeing you
could be like this.

Watching the moon
at dawn,
solitary, mid-sky,
I knew myself completely,
no part left out.

While many people stand watching the moon on a summer night, one hurries away . . .

Where
are you hurrying to?
You will see
the same moon tonight
wherever you go!

To a man who used to visit secretly but asked to come now in daylight

There are many
strange and lovely things
that swim in the midnight tide pools. . . .
I think I do not want to share them
with other divers' eyes by day.

When the autumn wind
blows down from Tokiwa Mountain,
my body fills, as if blushing,
with the color and scent
of pine.

I wonder
if the wind scythes a path
through my garden's wild grass
so someone can come
to visit?

[Written in response to Prince Atsumichi's first gift to Shikibu, a spray of orange blossoms sent without an accompanying poem]

Rather than recall
in these flowers
the fragrance of the past,
I would like to hear this nightingale's voice,
to know if his song is as sweet.

Nothing
in the world
is usual today.
This is
the first morning.

Come quickly—as soon as
these blossoms open,
they fall.
This world exists
as a sheen of dew on flowers.

Even though
these pine trees
keep their original color,
everything green
is different in spring.

Seeing you is the thread
that ties me to this life—
if that knot
were cut this moment,
I'd have no regret.

Yesterday,
what were my reasons
for sighing?
This morning,
love is more painful still.

Wishing to see him,
to be seen by him—
if only he
were the mirror
I face each morning.

Sleeplessly
I watch over
the spring night—
but no amount of guarding
is enough to make it stay.

On a night of bright moonlight, the prince came only to talk by my gatepost

If it rained now, perhaps,
this sky-crossing,
gate-passing
moon could be kept
from leaving. . . .

This heart is not
a summer field,
and yet . . .
how dense love's foliage
has grown.

Though I was expecting a visitor, he didn't arrive. Next morning, I sent this poem:

If I'd heard
so much as
a water rail's knock,
I'd have opened
the black pine door.

What is it
about this twilight hour?
Even the sound
of a barely perceptible breeze
pierces the heart.

If, however far away,
he were watching the lingering moon
with a heart at all like mine,
surely this clear sky
would be filled with clouds.

You ask my thoughts
through the long night?
I spent it listening
to the heavy rain
beating against the windows.

The dewdrop
on a bamboo leaf
stays longer
than you, who vanish
at dawn.

What is the use
of cherishing life in spring?
Its flowers
only shackle us
to this world.

This heart,
longing for you,
breaks
to a thousand pieces—
I wouldn't lose one.

More fragrant
because of the one
who saw and picked them,
these flowers,
precious, transient—

My lover, though he had broken off our affair, asked me not to replace the pillow we had slept on. My reply:

Well, just now I'm not sure
if I'll change my pillow
or not,
though I might decide
by watching you change your heart!

A man who hadn't visited for a long time finally came, but then didn't return

If you had
only stayed away
when I first missed you,
I might have forgotten
by now!

Waking up at dawn in November I heard a hard rain begin to fall

They say the winter days
are short,
but this one—
as soon as it grows light,
it grows dark!

All the flowers
have fallen in this wind
blowing through the night.
What will there be
for consolation tomorrow?

Watching the moon
at midnight . . .
I wonder
whose village
he watches it from.

If you and I had tied our vows
to the bush clover's leaves
I might hear
the sound of them loosening
in this autumn wind.

Even when a river of tears
courses through
this body,
the flame of love
cannot be quenched.

The cold rises
through the sleeve
of my pillowing arm—
I think that tonight
even my bed must frost.

A woman who has had many affairs gives birth to a child, and people ask who is the father. . . . Later, someone asks her how she decided. Her response:

In this world,
how can you know?
Soon enough you'll be able
to ask that dark one
who judges the past.

Reluctantly,
I too awaken—
the villagers
are pounding
their autumn clothes.

Even in my dreams
I never think of you—
how strange now,
seeing your handwriting,
to recall. . . .

An answer

Through the years
I've become used to sorrow:
there was not one spring
I didn't leave behind
the flowers.

Another answer

Do you not know
this world
is a waking dream?
However much I once needed you,
that is also a fleeting thing. . . .

Although the wind
blows terribly here,
the moonlight also leaks
between the roof planks
of this ruined house.

I used up this body
longing
for one who does not come.
A deep valley, now,
what once was my heart.

In my loneliness
I break and burn
twigs for the snapping fire—
in this wintry mountain village,
hoping the smoke at least won't leave.

When the netted fence of spiderwebs
that darkens my ruined house
can hold the wind in its strands—
that's when these troubled thoughts
will blow away. . . .

On the fifth day of the month, while offering incense at the front of the temple

My body's actions
speak of wanting to ride
a cloud to the Western Paradise—
why is it my heart
calls only North, towards you?

I think, "At least in my dreams
we'll be able to meet. . . ."
Moving my pillow
this way and that on the bed,
completely unable to sleep.

When the water-freezing
winter arrives,
the floating reeds look rooted,
as if stillness
were their own desire.

On New Year's Day, watching it snow

It seemed the plum trees
were already in bloom
but when I picked a branch
what fell—so much like flowers—
was snow.

If the one I've waited for
came now, what should I do?
This morning's garden filled with snow
is far too lovely
for footsteps to mar.

When we met again after a long separation, a man said that he could find nothing to say. My response:

Since nothing surpasses
seeing you,
no need for words.
Only concentrate on this,
on this. . . .

What color is
this blowing autumn wind,
that it can stain
my body
with its touch?

To a man who said he depended on me to think of him once in a while

Even if I
repeated love's name
forever,
could outward life match
the intensity of our hearts?

Someone asked to borrow a book, but as I hadn't made a copy for myself, I sent this poem instead:

We live
in a tide-swept inlet,
floating, flung.
In such a world, why cling to
collections of poems?

The one close to me now,
even my own body—
these too
will soon become clouds,
floating in different directions.

As I dig for wild orchids
in the autumn fields,
it is the deeply-bedded root
that I desire,
not the flower.

In the autumn, on retreat at a mountain temple

Although I try
to hold the single thought
of Buddha's teaching in my heart,
I cannot help but hear
the many crickets' voices calling as well.

On the night of the sixth, the sound of the night monk's voice reciting the Sutras mingled with the sound of incessant rain, and truly this seemed to be a world of dreams . . .

Should I leave this burning house
of ceaseless thought
and taste the pure rain's
single truth
falling upon my skin?

A string of jewels
from a broken necklace,
scattering—
more difficult to keep hold of
even than these is one's life.

On a troubled current
we grow old in this world—
today's rain-filled stream
will only increase
with tears.

Written when staying in a mountain temple

I've traveled
that dark path to the world
which comes down from this mountain
just to see you
one last time.

{Poems Mourning Prince Atsumichi}

Twilight,
and the path you took
coming and going from me
is also gone,
woven closed by spiderwebs and sorrow.

Too painful
that you became smoke—
even the cicada's
empty, useless shell
lasts on in existence.

{Poems Mourning Prince Atsumichi}

Remembering you. . . .
The fireflies of this marsh
seem like sparks
that rise
from my body's longing.

It would console me
if you returned
even for the length of the flash—
seen and then gone—
of lightning at dusk.

{Poems Mourning Prince Atsumichi}

For a moment,
he became smoke.
How intimate,
now,
the cloudy sky.

One by one,
at day's end,
the birds take flight
in all directions—
which could lead me to you?

{Poems Mourning Prince Atsumichi}

Those nights when we slept
behind love's
jeweled screen,
were we even aware of
the opening dawn skies?

Left behind
to grow old in this world
without you,
the flowers I pick lose their beauty,
dyed with dark ink.

{Poems Mourning Prince Atsumichi}

I long for the sound
of your voice.
The face
I see so clearly
doesn't say a word.

On the last night of the year, when the spirits of the dead return

Though they say
the dead come back tonight,
you are not here—
just my living village
without a soul.

{Poems Mourning Prince Atsumichi}

Written when thinking of becoming a nun

My body—
so used to you.
Even to think
of forgetting,
too sad to consider.

A friend, hearing I was in mourning, asked the cause of my grief

If I say
this or that,
how ordinary grief becomes—
broken cries are the words
that sorrow's voice demands.

{Poems Mourning Prince Atsumichi}

Again daylight
and I haven't joined him.
What should I do
with this body
that lives stubbornly on?

For his gaze,
it would have been clear:
the reflection
of this evening's moon,
clouding with tears in my eyes.

{Poems Mourning Prince Atsumichi}

If I live,
what more can I do?
Even the crickets
who don't know our world at all
cry and cry in autumn.

A friend asked to borrow the inkstone which had belonged to the prince

The past
is a subject
I cannot exhaust,
this inkstone
always wet with tears.

{Poems Mourning Prince Atsumichi}

My body, wandering, lost,
knows only night now—
that is why my sleeves
stay soaked in darkness,
unable to dry.

{Poems Mourning Naishi}

Around the time Naishi {Shikibu's daughter} died, snow fell, then melted away

Why did you vanish
into empty sky?
Even the fragile snow,
when it falls,
falls in this world.

During the memorial service for my daughter

Listen, listen:
longing and loss.
In the struck bell's
recurrent calling,
no moment in which to forget.

The usual period of mourning is over,
and I must take off
these dark wisteria-cloth robes.
What I wear from today will be dyed
only with tears.

When I was thinking not to age any longer in this world, I saw a small child

It is easy
to hate this painful world,
but how can I leave
a world
that includes this child?

Perhaps, if I make a friend
of the mountain cuckoo
in this world,
he will talk with me
when we cross the mountain of death.

[This is believed to have been Shikibu's final poem, written on her deathbed]

The way I must enter
leads through darkness to darkness—
O moon above the mountains' rim,
please shine a little further
on my path.

APPENDIX

ON JAPANESE POETRY AND THE PROCESS OF TRANSLATION

For those who may wish to know a bit more about Japanese poetry and the language in which these poems were written, this appendix provides a brief introduction, as well as a few examples of the process underlying the translation. In addition, the curious can turn to the notes to individual poems, which include the *romaji* (the Japanese text written in roman alphabet) for each poem, offer specific background information when it might be of interest, point out the use of certain technical devices, and, occasionally, expand on a poem's meaning or highlight its technique.

Of the many differences between the language in which these poems were composed and that into which they have come, one of the most significant is that Heian-era Japanese (and present-day Japanese) is a highly inflected language. This means that grammatical constructions are often contained within the words themselves, usually in their endings, as in Latin; when an auxiliary word is used, it generally follows rather than precedes its companion. English, by comparison, is a partially inflected language; although some information is given in word endings—for example, the distinction between singular and plural—word order also greatly determines grammar. "The man ate the lion" means something quite different from "the lion ate the man."

Because of the conventions of ordering in English grammar, the understanding of a sentence tends to develop from beginning to end, and when auxiliary words are used ("I will have left by then"), they generally precede the part of speech they modify. For novice readers of Japanese, the order in which a poem's information unfolds, both within phrases and over the course of the poem, at first often seems reversed. Again, anyone who has studied Latin or another inflected language knows how quickly one learns to take one's cues as they come; but until the originals' order begins to seem natural, reading the phrases backwards word by word or starting the poem from its end will usually help in untangling the meaning. (An additional source of potential confusion is the fact that the language of the Heian era differs more greatly from contemporary Japanese than that of Chaucer from contemporary English, and some of the words in these poems were archaic even at the time of composition.)

Differences in linguistic structure between English and Japanese also affect sound qualities, both within words and in the way sound functions in poetry. It is not at all unusual, for example, for a Japanese word to occupy seven syllables; *onomatopoeia*, an exceptionally many-syllabled word for English, has only six syllables.* Also, the fact that all words in Japanese end with one of a relatively small number of vowels (plus the occasional word ending with *n*, which is counted as a syllable and derives from the older *mu*) precludes the use of rhyme as it is employed in other languages: only a large variety of possible end-sounds allows their duplication to become a source of ingenuity and surprise, and, hence, aesthetic pleasure.

Several other important differences between the two languages are worth noting. A Japanese poet may choose to specify a pronoun, verb

**In the* romaji *in this book, many of these multisyllabled words have been broken into their component parts, although in the Japanese they are more like a continuous series of suffixes. (See page 177 for a further description of the* romaji.*)*

tense, or whether a noun is singular or plural, but very often such information is not given; in Japanese, nouns are not accompanied by modifying articles such as *the* or *a*, *this* or *whose*. These constructions are not needed for the Japanese poems to be clear to their readers, but in bringing such poems into English, certain choices may have to be made simply because of the nature of the language. In English, for example, a poem almost always needs to be put into a grammatical voice; in this book, the choice has usually been first person or second person for a poem without a specified speaker or point of view, according to which seemed most true to the spirit of the original as well as most aesthetically effective in the new version.

It should be pointed out that these grammatical differences, which are to some extent mirrored in cultural differences, give the poems a broadly different quality in translation than they have in the original. In the Japanese, it is the experience itself, not the subjective frame around it, that is offered in a poem and felt to be important. The author and the reader of a poem are less separated when there is no specified *I*, *you*, or *he* to "own" the experience being spoken of, and the ambiguity of situation which is inherent in certain poems is a source of increased resonance and richness for the reader, not confusion. One of the great strengths of Japanese poetry is precisely this power to work through suggestion, to present in a few lightly sketched phrases an image that can be both emotionally evocative and metaphysically profound.

Although Japanese poetic diction is sometimes vague about situational specifics, it contains a wealth of words that communicate the feeling with which one is to understand a poem. These intensifying particles make for subtle shifts in emotion that the writer in English can only attempt to recreate in punctuation and rhythm, and in the choice of words; what is lost in this process is the particular visibility of the choice of feeling in the Japanese, the highly orchestrated flow of murmur and exclamation. (Or, if *zo*, for example, is rendered by an exclamation point, we can see how English uses heard shifts in pitch—an exclamation point is essentially a musical notation—to accomplish what Japanese, in its relatively unstressed verbal flow, uses a word to communicate.

Certain problematic words come up again and again in the translation of Japanese, the most common of which is *aware*. Something *aware* might be "sorrowful," "loving," "beautiful," "interesting," "tasteful," "regretful," "nostalgic," "graceful," "delicious"—virtually any adjective for which the feeling of the poem and its contextual situation might call. The word also sometimes appears not as an adjective but as a kind of exclamation or verbal sigh, a general summing up of the author's feeling about the contents of the poem. Most of the time, *aware* signifies a complex mixture of emotions, rather like a well-cooked soup, but at its core it embodies the recognition and appreciation of beauty mixed with transience. The closest English equivalent to *aware*'s central meaning is *poignant*, in its meaning of "emotionally moving," but that word is too formal and stiffly self-conscious to our ears to offer itself very gracefully for use in a poem.

Completely lost to translation is the fact that every author and reader of these poems held in mind and heart a vast anthology of earlier poems and the associations they evoked. Certain places are rich in literary history; mentioning them called up in the reader the exact words and emotions of prior works, and one's own poem was perceived in the light of this continuous exchange and dialogue with the past. Phrases from earlier poems would be used in one's own, sometimes with only the smallest variations. This was not plagiarism—when the same body of knowledge is available to everyone, everyone can be expected to recognize a source—but a proper and effective use of one of the available instruments for increasing resonance and meaning. Thus, an interwoven language of allusion and evocation linked these small poems to a great web of shared culture and understanding.

And these poems are small. Each *tanka*, as this verse form which dominated Japanese poetry for a thousand years is called, consists of thirty-one syllables, arranged in a metric pattern of 5–7–5–7–7. There are no stresses within the lines. (The term *lines* is used here to indicate the above metrical units; the poems were originally written without the physical line breaks that readers have come to consider the main typographical indication that a poem is in fact a poem.) As mentioned earlier, there is no rhyme scheme, although the sound of words was employed for its emotional power and resonance in much the same way sound is used in contemporary American free verse. (Some scholars believe that there may have been conventions governing vowel arrangements, but I am not familiar with them. There are, however, poems in which repetitions of sound, a kind of internal rhyme, can be clearly heard.)

For those who wish to attempt to read the *romaji* in the notes to the poems, vowels in Japanese are pronounced like the vowels in Italian, consonants as in English (the *g* is always hard), and every vowel is pronounced. For the purpose of metrical counting, vowels with a macron above them are held for two beats, an *n* at the end of a word, as mentioned earlier, is usually counted as a beat, and very occasionally two adjacent vowels are elided into a single syllable. For the most part, the units of meter are also units of meaning, but enjambment (if it may be called that) is far from rare; a break in thought or grammar often occurs between the third and fourth lines of the poem.

To give some fuller sense of the way these poems function in the original, and also to offer the reader a feel for the kinds of decisions that were made in these particular translations, a few examples follow; they are transcribed in the form that Mariko Aratani and I used to set up our work. First is one by Izumi Shikibu in which the task of translation was quite straightforward:

NADOTE KIMI / MUNASHIKI SORA NI / KIE NI KEN /
why you empty sky in disappear did (?)

AWAYUKI DANI MO / HURE BA HURU YO NI
frail snow even ! falling when falling world in

With very little effort, this poem quickly yields its meaning. (A prose headnote—not uncommon in Japanese poetry—gives more information about the poem's background: "Around the time Naishi [Shikibu's daughter] died, snow fell, then melted away.")

> Why did you vanish
> into empty sky?
> Even the fragile snow,
> when it falls,
> falls in this world.

In this small poem of mourning, some of the means by which Japanese poetry attains remarkable emotional depth within a brief utterance can be seen. There is the all-pervasive device of intertwining human and natural worlds, in which the natural illuminates the human to keenly felt effect. There is the two-phase rhetoric, in which occurs the movement of human heart and mind that is essential to any good poem. There is the reticence of the emotion, the way deep feeling lies under seemingly straightforward visual description (cremation was the usual manner of handling the body after death; hence, one literally "vanished into empty sky"). And there is the emotion itself, in this case the double-edged use of the Buddhist concept of transience: acknowledged as the true course of things (no one would ask snow not to fall, or melt), the fact of transience is still piercingly, painfully experienced (however briefly the snow falls, it can still be seen for its moment and will return; Naishi has utterly disappeared). The best-known, simplest, and perhaps most moving example of this dual relationship to transience is a haiku by the eighteenth-century poet Issa, written after the death of *his* daughter:

This dewdrop world:
It is a dewdrop world . . .
And yet, and yet—

In the next poem, by Ono no Komachi, somewhat more liberty was needed to bring the emotional impact across in English:

ITO	*SEMETE*	/	*KOISHIKI*	*TOKI*	*WA*	/	*UBATAMA*	*NO* /
very	extremely		longing	time	—		hiougi nut	's

YORU	*NO*	*KOROMO*	*O*	/	*KAESHITE*	*ZO*	*KIRU*
night	's	clothing	(obj.)		turned inside out	!	wear

The most notable feature of this poem is Komachi's willingness to reveal personal passion; it also demonstrates one of the primary technical devices of Japanese poetry, the *makurakotoba*, or pillow word. The poem—as do so many of her poems—shows Komachi alone and missing an unnamed lover. A subject which occurs again and again in her work is her response to seeing her lover in a dream—in one poem she wishes she had never wakened; in another she decides to commit herself to a life of dreaming; in a third she mourns the cruelty of the fact that even in their dream meetings she and her lover fear being seen. In this poem, however, we see her awake, following the folk custom of turning one's nightgown inside out—this, like the American custom of slipping a piece of wedding cake under a pillow, was believed to make one dream of one's love.

Here is the version of the poem in this book:

> When my desire
> grows too fierce
> I wear my bed clothes
> inside out,
> dark as the night's rough husk.

The opening phrase of the original is, to contemporary American ears, abstract rather than emotional, so I decided to attempt to render its intention rather than its literal meaning. A phrase such as *ito semete* ("very extremely") is quite unusual in *tanka*; later in the poem, the word *zo* also functions as an intensifier. My response was to replace the usual translation of *koishiki*, "longing," with the stronger phrasing of fierce desire. Although the translation, like the poem itself, doesn't offer any explanation for the custom of reversing one's clothes, I added an element of causality by beginning the poem with *When*. And I tried to give the pillow word, *ubatama*, an extra imagistic vividness and weight. A pillow word is a phrase that is traditionally coupled with its noun, much like a Homeric epithet (*wine-dark* sea, for example). Many pillow words seem baffling to present-day readers, or their meanings are simply not known, and some scholars omit them from translation. Yet clearly this is an unfortunate practice: an accomplished poet would only use a pillow word for good reason. One possible reason would be to enrich the sensuality of the poem; another would be to evoke the emotional resonance of these ancient phrases. Researching *ubatama*, a pillow word for night, I learned that the hiougi nut has a virtually black shell; I then made rather free with the image to create the last line of this version.

One thing the process of translation teaches is that other choices could always have been made. One alternative translation for this poem is

> Longing,
> fiercely longing—
> To dream of him
> I turn my bed clothes inside out
> this dark-husked night.

A final example of the process underlying these translations is another poem of Komachi's. One of her most famous, it illustrates a further device in Japanese poetry, the *kakekotoba*, or pivot-word, a word which contains two different meanings, each fully intended to function as part of the poem's imagery and content.

HANA	*NO*	*IRO*	*WA*	/	*UTSURI*	*NI*	*KERI*	*NA*	/	*ITAZURA*	*NI*	/
flower	's	color	(subj.)		faded	has	alas			uselessly		

WAGA	*MI*	*YO*	*NI*	*HURU*	/	*NAGAME*	*SESHI*	*MA*	*NI*
my	body	world	in	aging		long rains	doing		while
				*		*			
				falling		watching			

In this poem Komachi confronts transience in a manner quite different from Shikibu's in her poem of mourning for her daughter—here it is the poet's own relationship to time which is being explored:

While watching
the long rains falling on this world
my heart, too, fades
with the unseen color
of the spring flowers.

The heart of this poem is its complex and skillful interweaving of the various images of passing time. No translation can convey *kakekotoba* with justice, and it is probable that no one from a different culture can fully appreciate the depth of regret expressed in Komachi's image of uselessly fading spring flowers. Whereas a poet of ancient Rome responded to transience and mortality with the proud refusal of *carpe diem*, the Heian poet acquiesced to it with a heart full of sorrow and deep feeling, and knew that such feeling was the true mark of being human. In this translation the idea of aging is implied rather than directly stated, but in the original the adjacent pivot-words *huru* and *nagame*, with their multiple readings, create a kind of harmonic resonance between themselves: the poet is growing old as it rains, she is watching her own aging, the long rains are inexorably falling. In a mingling of subjective and objective worlds, the poet looks out her window on a rain which causes flowers to fade without being viewed, as she herself grows older without being known by her lover. It is the other side of Komachi's passionate dream life we see in this poem, the long hours of waking and solitude, the realization that human life is fleeting and the pleasures of youth and beauty even more fleeting.

When it comes to the issue of how best to fulfill the ideal of faithfulness in terms of a poem's formal structure, each translator will have different replies to the same questions. Usually, as is clear from the preceding examples, my own inclination is not to be inflexibly committed to re-creating the formal properties of the original in a time of free verse—mostly because I think it is in the subtle parts of a poem's use of sound that its musical genius is likely to lie. Though the form as a whole is a quintessential part of a poem's mode of thought, to reproduce the outer form strictly but coarsely, meanwhile distorting the meaning, can be more of a disservice to that thought than the failure to attempt its communication at all. Too often the effort to preserve exactly thirty-one syllables in the translation of *tanka* results in either a poem with words added merely to fill out the count or one with part of its meaning or imagery left out. Furthermore, the powerful aural resonance of the form itself, built up by long familiarity with its use in the responses of a Japanese reader, is nonexistent for one brought up on the meters and forms of English and European poetry. But, while I don't feel it important to duplicate the exact syllabic count of Japanese poetry, I am always surprised if a three-line haiku appears as a couplet, or a five-line *waka* (the other name sometimes used for the *tanka* form) is made into a quatrain. Rather than experiencing these English forms as somehow "equivalent," I find that the essentially asymmetrical nature of the original is lost by turning to what may seem to be the nearest convention, and that the use of our own convention masks the nature of the original poems, making them seem less different in rhythm and approach than they are. Yet clearly many very fine translators, from both ends of the spectrum of freedom and form, disagree with my reactions.

Anyone who attempts that impossible task, the translation of poetry, must at some point wonder what exactly a poem might be, if not its own body of words. For surely, as all can attest who have made the hard and joyous effort to write well a poem of their own, poetry dwells in words: absolutely particular in meaning, irreplaceably individual in rhythm and sound. Yet there must be something in addition to words, an underlying sense of a destination unknown but also *there*, which makes us accept one phrase and reject another when they rise to mind in a poem's first making, or delete or alter or add when we revise. The act of writing a poem is not only a making but also a following: of the mystery of source as it emerges into form, of the wisdom of the heart and mind as it encounters the wisdom of language. The act of translation constitutes a leap of faith, a belief that somehow this part of a poem that lives both through words and beyond words can be kept alive, can move from its life in one verbal body into another.

All translations are inescapably ephemeral, linked to the poetry of their own time's language in a way that an original work is not. Yet most of us depend on translations—if we are lucky, in several versions—as the only way to encounter the poetry of other cultures and times. In the old teaching story, each of a group of blind men touches a different part of an elephant and describes his findings about this strange animal to the others: "long and thin as a rope," reports the man grasping the tail; "broad and rough as the trunk of a tree," says the one encountering a leg; "hard and smooth as a curved sword," announces the one touching the tusk. The translations in this book can convey only a similar, partial, idea of Komachi's and Shikibu's work. But the elephant lives on in its own nature, regardless of our ideas.

The ninth-century Japanese Buddhist monk Kūkai—in legend, the man responsible for developing *kana*, the system for using Chinese written characters to convey Japanese words, which enabled the Heian-era court women to transcribe their poems—wrote a quatrain about the way source travels out into multitudinous form, always changing, shifting, illuminating:

SINGING IMAGE OF FIRE

A hand moves, and the fire's whirling takes different
    shapes,
triangles, squares: all things change when we do.
The first word, *Ah*, blossomed into all others.
Each of them is true.

In the spirit of this poem, greatly encouraging to poets and greatly encouraging to translators, we offer the work in this book.

JH

NOTES TO THE POEMS

About the *romaji*: The textual source for the poems translated in this book is *Izumi Shikibu Shū / Ono no Komachi Shū*, edited by Utsubo Kubota (Tokyo: Asahi Shimbunsha, Nihon Koten Zensho, 1958). All the *romaji* in this book are the work of Mariko Aratani. Because there is no exact equivalence between written Japanese and written English, various methods of transliteration into the roman alphabet exist. Here, the general principles were (1) to have the written versions correspond as closely as possible to the sound of the poems as they would now be spoken; (2) when dealing with grammatical elements which are not, when written in Japanese characters, clearly one word or two, to separate them in the *romaji* in a way that would correspond to the reader's sense of what constitutes a word. An example of the first guideline is the use of *hu* for the syllable usually transcribed as *fu*; an example of the latter is the separation in these written versions of *ba*, meaning "since," "if," or "when," from the body of the verb it governs. We have also used the English poetic convention of dividing metrical units into poetic "lines" by slash marks, though in Japanese the poems are not divided in any fixed manner when written. For scholars, we trust the *romaji* will serve primarily as a means of identifying the original poems. For nonreaders of Japanese, we hope they will allow some access, however limited, to the prosody and music of Komachi's and Shikibu's work.

NOTES TO KOMACHI'S POEMS

p. 5: *Omoi tsutsu / nure baya hito no / mietsu ran /*
yume to shirise ba / samezara mashi o

Komachi's poems of desire introduced a new voice into Japanese poetry. Never before had personal passion been given so direct an expression; many of the best women poets of later ages, including Izumi Shikibu, clearly followed a path first blazed by Komachi. This poem introduces a quintessential theme in Komachi's work, which recurs over and over: unfulfilled passion and longing, as experienced in both waking life and dream. The poet, unable to see her lover because of circumstances that are never explained in the poems, seems to think of him without respite, whether sleeping or lying awake through long nights as she wonders if he will appear. One may conjecture that there was a great difference in rank between the lovers, that he was away from the capital much of the time, or simply (though one hopes this was not the case) that this unnamed person cared a good deal less for Komachi than she did for him.

Beyond the fierce intensity of their content, many of Komachi's poems also demonstrate in the original a remarkable complexity of technique; no poet has used the *kakekotoba*, or pivot-word (see Appendix, page 171), to greater effect. It is as if the strength and depth of Komachi's emotion press against the *tanka* form itself until the imagery bursts, virtually literally, through the poems' thirty-one syllables.

A final quality to be noted in Komachi's poems of desire is the way her exploration of personal emotion often (though not always) leads to an exploration of the metaphysical. The relationship between dream life and waking life; inquiry into this thing called "reality"; recognition of the discrepancy between outer appearance and inner truth—all these are matters not only of erotic love but of every aspect of human existence. Komachi's genius was to demonstrate in her work that to investigate any feeling sufficiently deeply is to reach down to the very bedrock of our lives.

p. 6: *Ito semete / koishiki toki wa / ubatama no /*
yoru no koromo o / kaeshite zo kiru

See the Appendix, page 169, for a full discussion of this poem. A slightly different version uses the verb *sleep* in place of *wear*.

p. 7: *Kagiri naki / omoi no mama ni / yoru mo kon /*
yumeji o sae ni / hito wa togameji

p. 8: *Hito ni awan / tsuki no naki yo wa / omoiokite /*
mune hashiribi ni / kokoro yake ori

This poem, one of Komachi's most famous, and the most powerful example of her mastery of pivot-words, possesses an intensity of intermingling images quite impossible to convey in translation. The first pivot-word is *tsuki*, which means both "moon" and "way." The night without a moon is also a night without a way to see her lover; from this double reading of one word emerges the image of a night so dark a man could not find his way to her door. Much of the fire imagery of the rest of the poem also comes from pivot-words, rising into the poem's meaning in much the way firelight reaches up into the darkness of the room where the poet lies awake, thinking of her lover. The fire that burns in the midst of the words which also show the poet thinking is both inner and outer (we know from other Heian poems that the poet was likely to have had an actual charcoal brazier in her room); the interplay between the blazing of her body and the image of a small, sputtering brazier surrounded by the night's darkness creates in the reader an awareness of the poem's intense subjectivity. Further, we see the flame of the poet's desire as the only waking activity in a world swallowed by blackness—true cause for despair.

p. 9: *Utsutsu niwa / samo koso arame / yume ni sae /*
hitome tsutsumu to / miru ga wabishiki

This poem exists in two versions. In one, the dream lovers "wrap people's eyes" (the literal reading of *hitome tsutsumu*, meaning "to conceal"); in the other, they "fear" people's eyes.

p. 10: *Yumeji niwa / ashi mo yasumezu / kayoe domo /*
utsutsu ni hitome / mishi koto wa arazu

p. 11: *Tsuma kouru / saoshika no ne ni / sayo hukete /*
waga katakoi o / ari to shirinuru

p. 12: *Yume nara ba / mata miru kai mo / arina mashi /*
nani nakanaka no / utsutsu naru ran

p. 13: *Higurashi no / naku yamazato no / yūgure wa /*
kaze yori hoka ni / tou hito zo naki

p. 14: *Mirume ara ha / uramin ya wa to / ama iwa ba /*
ukabite matan / utakata no mi mo

Mirume, a favorite image and pivot-word of Komachi's, means both "seaweed" and "eyes of seeing," as in seeing, or meeting, a lover. This is a rather free translation of a poem which depends on both this and another play on words. Literally, though still somewhat simplified, it says, "Does a diver say she'll turn against a bay in which there is seaweed [and does a lover resent one who wishes to see him]? No. I will wait, floating, also a body of sea foam."

p. 15: *Hitorine no / wabishiki mama ni / okii tsutsu /*
tsuki o aware to / imi zo kanetsuru

Two differing prose headnotes offer background for this poem. In one version, Komachi is alone because it is a night when according to religious custom one must be; her lover has come to spy on her, and, seeing her out gazing at the moon, sends a note quoting an ancient poem which says that on such a night moon gazing as well is taboo. In the other, it is a former lover who sends a note objecting to her admiring the moon. In either case, Komachi's reply is firm—deprived of love, she will not also deprive herself of the moon's companionship.

p. 16: *Yo no naka wa / yume ka utsutsu ka / utsutsu to mo /*
yume to mo shirazu / arite nakere ba

Yo no naka means literally "the world of the middle." The reference can be either to the human world or to the world of relationship and love. This poem is deeply Buddhist in its questioning of what, if anything, can be called "real."

p. 17: *Momiji senu / Tokiwa no yama wa / huku kaze no /*
oto ni ya aki o / kikiwataru ran

Literally, the poem says that Tokiwa Mountain does not change color. The reason for this—it is covered with pine trees—is only implied, but Komachi would have expected all readers of this poem to have known the mountain from their own experience. The idea behind one of her most powerful poems, "*Iro miede . . .*" (see page 46), is also seen here—a poignant recognition that while change is inevitably running its course, the appearance of things can remain the same. Autumn, in this poem, might refer to the end of a relationship or perhaps to the coming of old age—while the poet's eye is ostensibly turned outward, it is in the meeting of the heart's experience and the phenomena of the outer world that Japanese poetry lives. (See Ki no Tsurayuki's statement in the Introduction, page xix.)

p. 18: *Itsu tote mo / koishi karazu wa / arane domo /*
ayashi kari keru / aki no yūgure

p. 19: *Hukimusubu / kaze wa mukashi no / aki nagara /*
arishi nimo niru / sode no tsuyu kana

The "entangling" (*hukimusubu*) wind of this poem is, literally, a "blowing-and-tying" wind; Komachi may have invented this word. One thinks of all things being connected, almost by accident, by the pervasive wind's gusts, while only the poet is left unattached. One thinks also of the ties of karma, for the poet's tears show that she is still connected, if only to the past. The interplay of old and new, lasting and impermanent, is filled with a delicate irony—the poet's sleeves the year before would also have been damp, with the autumn dew of secret meetings by dark.

p. 20: *Sora o iku / tsuki no hikari o / kumoi yori /*
mide ya yami nite / yo wa hatenu beki

This poem shows Komachi flirtatiously (albeit anonymously) issuing a romantic proposition of her own. While many of her best poems depict Komachi rather hopelessly waiting for the lover she rarely sees, this and several others show her as a woman confident of her desirability—one who can tease, solicit, and even reject members of the opposite sex. This side of her personality has rarely appeared in English anthologies, but it forms a major part of Komachi's legend in Japan, where many stories show her in later years atoning for the pride and cruelty of her youth.

p. 21: *Aki no yo mo / na nomi nari keri / Ai to ae ba /*
koto zo to mo naku / ake nuru mono o

As discussed in the Introduction, a lover would come secretly to a woman's chamber after dark and leave again before dawn. In this poem it is clear that the two become so enraptured in seeing each other and talking that morning arrived before they had the chance to consummate their meeting.

p. 22: *Shidoke naki / nuku taregami o / miseji tote /*
hata kakuretaru / kesa no asagao

So few of Komachi's poems allow us a glimpse of her feeling happiness in love that it is pleasant to contemplate what circumstances might have led to this charming poem.

p. 23: *Iwa no ue ni / tabine o sure ba / ito samushi /*
koke no koromo o / ware ni kasanan

Yo o somuku / koke no koromo wa / tada hitoe /
kasane ba utoshi / iza hutari nen

One may reach what conclusion one wishes about this poetic dialogue!

p. 24: *Wasuregusa / wagami ni tsuman to / omoishi o /*
hito no kokoro ni / ouru nari keri

Wasuregusa, the Japanese "forgetting grass," is, oddly, virtually a mirror image of our forget-me-nots. Touching though the situation of this poem is, there is also a wry humor in its self-deprecation.

p. 25: *Kokoro kara / ukitaru hune ni / norisomete /*
hitohi mo nami ni / nurenu hi zo naki

Like the preceding poem, this one offers a glimpse of Komachi examining her all-too-usual situation with both honesty and humor.

p. 26: *Mirume naki / wagami o ura to / shirane ba ya /*
karenade ama no / ashi tayuku kuru

This poem uses the same imagery and pivot-words as the one on page 14 (seaweed and seeing a lover; a bay and resentment in love; the figure of a diver), but to very different effect and purposes. In this case the man is a diver who won't give up his approaches, although the poet has attempted to make clear that she has no wish to see him; her body is "a bay without seaweed."

p. 27: *Tomo sure ba / ada naru kaze ni / sazanami no /*
nabiku chō goto / ware nabike to ya

Chō is written "tefu."

p. 28: *Hana sakite / mi naranu mono wa / wadatsumi no /*
kazashi ni saseru / oki no shiranami

This poem has something of the quality of an artist's quick sketch.

p. 29: *Yoso ni koso / mine no shirakumo to / omoishi ni /*
hutari ga naka ni / haya tachi ni keri

A somewhat different version of this poem also exists. One tradition has it that the poem was written, when Komachi was quite young, upon the death of her grandmother.

p. 30: *Aware nari / wagami no hate ya / asamidori /*
tsui niwa nobe no / kasumi to omoe ba

p. 31: *Harusame no / sawa ni huru goto / oto mo naku /*
hito ni shirarede / nururu sode kana

p. 32: *Katami koso / ima wa ada nare / kore naku ba /*
wasururu toki mo / ara mashi mono o

p. 33: *Wagami koso / aranu ka to nomi / tadorarure /*
tou beki hito ni / wasurareshi yori

p. 34: *Kasumi tatsu / no o natsukashimi / harukoma no /*
arete mo kimi ga / miyuru koro kana

Arete mo, "becoming wild," also means "growing distant."

p. 35: *Suma no ama no / ura kogu hune no / kaji o tae / yorubé naki mi zo / kanashi kari keru*

p. 36: *Konoma yori / morikuru tsuki no / kage mire ba / kokorozukushi no / aki wa kini keri*

p. 37: *Dare o kamo / Matsuchi no yama no / ominaeshi / aki to chigireru / hito zo aru rashi*

Although many poems that use puns on place names prove difficult to translate, Waiting Mountain is instantly comprehensible in this one.

p. 38: *Akikaze ni / au tanomi koso / kanashi kere / wagami munashiku / narinu to omoe ba*

The final three lines of this poem (which, in the order of thought in English, are the statement's beginning) read "It is sorrowful, when I think that my body has become empty . . ." The other two lines contain two pivot-words: the word for autumn, *aki*, can also be the word for the feeling of satiety, meaning that Komachi's lover has tired of her; and *tanomi*, grain (literally, "fruit of the field"), can also mean "to depend upon" or "to expect." Thus, what is sorrowful is both the grain as it encounters the autumn winds and the fact that the poet desires to keep seeing a man who has tired of the relationship. In this imagery of the end of love, youth, and summer's fruitfulness, the world of the poet's own body and that of nature intermingle in a complex yet seamless statement of despair. The translation is a somewhat free attempt to convey all these aspects of the poem with something of the wholeness of the original, taking the introductory headnote into account.

p. 39: *Ima wa tote / wagami shigure ni / hurinure ba /*
koto no ha sae ni / utsuroi ni keri

p. 40: *Yamazato wa / mono no sabishiki / koto koso are /*
yo no uki yori wa / sumiyo kari keri

This poem is surely one source for the legends that portray Komachi ending her years deep in the mountains, leading a life of Buddhist austerity and detachment.

p. 41: *Momokusa no / hana no himo toku / aki no no ni /*
omoitawaren / hito na togame so

This poem seems a likely source for the Nō play *Komachi at Sekidera* (see Introduction, page xxiii), at the end of which the poet performs what was traditionally a young boy's ritual dance. The play, however, depicts Komachi as ashamed of her inappropriate display, whereas the poem seems to show more a free-spirited independence from the conventions of behavior in old age.

p. 42: *Mono o koso / iwane no matsu mo / omou rame /*
chiyo huru sue mo / katabuki ni keri

How delicately, in describing an ancient, bowed-down pine, Komachi offers this self-portrait of old age; only the single word *mo* ("too") directs the reader to the poem's subjective aspect. Or, from a different perspective, one can admire this poem as a demonstration of the way long suffering can bring up a deeply Buddhist empathy with the suffering of all beings, even trees; considered this way, the poem's movement is from the inner world to the outer, from the personal to the universal.

p. 43: *Ogurayama / kieshi tomoshi no / koe mo gana /*
shika narawazu ba / yasuku nena mashi

A fairly free translation. Literally, this poem's meaning is "I might sleep easily if only I hadn't learned to listen this way for the deer's calling [to begin] after the [hunting] lanterns on Mount Ogura have gone out."

p. 44: *Wabinure ba / mi o ukikusa no / ne o taete /*
sasou mizu ara ba / inan to zo omou

This is one of Komachi's best-known poems.

p. 45: *Hana no iro wa / utsuri ni keri na / itazura ni /*
wagami yo ni huru / nagame seshi ma ni

See the Appendix (page 172) for an in-depth discussion of this poem. Keen-eyed readers may notice a sixth syllable in the first line of this *tanka*; one may assume that, as in Latin scansion, the two adjacent vowels of *no iro* can be elided in the count.

p. 46: *Iro miede / utsurou mono wa / yo no naka no /*
hito no kokoro no / hana ni zo ari keku

This poem, also one of Komachi's most famous, is usually read as alluding specifically to love, a commentary on the way passion can fade without leaving any mark on the lover's outward appearance; various words which are by custom associated with one another and with love, as well as the phrase *yo no naka* (discussed in the note to page 16), point to this reading. Yet this poem can also be taken as a statement about the nature of change in general—in the world of nature, change is accompanied by outward signs, whereas in human beings the feeling heart continually changes quite invisibly; thus, human emotion is even less permanent or trustworthy than any other natural phenomenon. Here, as in many of her best poems, when Komachi dwells on the nature of love at its deepest, she makes her home in the realm of larger questions.

p. 47: *Aru wa naku / naki wa kazu sou / yo no naka ni /*
aware izure no / hi made nagekan

p. 48: *Yamazato no / aretaru yado o / terashi tsutsu /*
ikuyo henu ran / aki no tsukikage

The abandoned house in this poem is surely a figure for the self at last free from any concept of self, and the moon is a symbol for Buddhist enlightenment. What emerges is, once again, a powerful image of the poet in solitary old age: having abandoned, or been abandoned by, the world of her fellows, Komachi remains awake in the long autumn night, illuminated now not by the burning passions of her earlier poems but by moonlight—the vast and shining salvation of the Way, whose nights on earth cannot be counted.

NOTES TO SHIKIBU'S POEMS

p. 51: *Kurokami no / midare mo shirazu / uchihuse ba /*
mazu kakiyarishi / hito zo koishiki

Shikibu's tangled black hair in this poem is often referred to by scholars as one of the very few examples in Japanese poetry of a specific reference to the poet's own body. This phrase was again made famous more recently, when the best-known Japanese feminist poet of the twentieth century, Yosano Akiko, took *Tangled Hair* for a book title.

p. 52: *Omoiki ya / arite wasurenu / ono ga mi o /*
kimi ga katami ni / nasan to omoe ba

p. 53: *Yo no naka ni / koi to iu iro wa / nakere domo /*
hukaku mi ni shimu / mono ni zo arikeru

p. 54: *Ume ga ka ni / odorokare tsutsu / haru no yo no /*
yami koso hito wa / akugarashi kere

p. 55: *Hito no mi mo / koi niwa kaetsu / natsumushi no /*
arawa ni moyu to / mienu bakari zo

p. 56: *Kaku bakari / shinoburu ame o / hito towa ba /*
nani ni nuretaru / sode to iuran

p. 57: *Yoyo o hete / ware ya wa / mono o omou beki /*
tada hitotabi no / au koto ni yori

This may be the most graceful letter of rejection ever sent: although Shikibu is turning down the man's invitation, she gives as her reason that to meet even once would be so extraordinary that for many lifetimes to come she would be left hoping to repeat the experience.

p. 58: *Iro ni idete / hito ni kataru na / murasaki no /*
nezuri no koromo / kite netariki to

One cannot help but think that the intention of this poem, with its overt allusion to a purple root, was to cause the very blush it cautions against. So many poems were written to be sent along with items of clothing forgotten by lovers (presumably in the darkness and haste of predawn departures) that they constitute a virtual subgenre of love poetry.

p. 59: *Waga yado no / momiji no nishiki / ika ni shite /*
kokoro yasuku wa / tatsu ni ka aru ran

The homonym in the English of this poem, the plural of *leaf* and the verb *leaving*, echoes a doubling in the Japanese, in which *tatsu* is a pivot-word meaning "cut" and "leave."

p. 60: *Iwatsutsuji / orimote zo miru / seko ga kishi /*
kurenaizome no / kinu ni nitare ba

p. 61: *Masazama ni / sakura mo sakan / mi niwa min /*
kokoro ni ume no / ka o ba shinobite

Clearly the reference in this poem is to a relationship which took place when the plums were in blossom; the poem is a classic example of the way human affairs are depicted in Japanese poetry by imagery taken wholly from nature.

p. 62: *Hana chirasu / haru no arashi wa / akikaze no /*
mi ni shimu yori mo / wabishi kari keri

Comparison of the relative merits of the seasons—almost always spring and autumn—was one of the most time honored and frequent topics in classical Japanese literature; in this poem, Shikibu makes the case for spring. As always, one must consider what human events and feelings might correspond to the seasonal imagery.

p. 63: *Hodo hure ba / hito wa wasurete / yami ni ken /*
chigirishi koto o / nao tanomu kana

p. 64: *Shiratsuyu mo / yume mo kono yo mo / maboroshi mo /*
tatoete ie ba / hisashi kari keri

In the original, the word *love* is left unspoken.

p. 65: *Aware to mo / iwamashi mono o / hito no seshi /*
akatsukioki wa / kurushi kari keru

Although usually a man came to the woman's home, in this case the lovers slept elsewhere. This is Shikibu's commentary on the actuality—as opposed to the observation—of early rising and travel. Refreshingly tart, it shows her customary faithfulness to the true nature of her experience.

p. 66: *Natsugoromo / kite wa miene do / waga tame ni /*
usuki kokoro no / arawa naru kana

p. 67: *Hakanaku mo / wasurare ni keru / Ōgi kana /*
ochi tari keri to / hito mo koso mire

This poem and the next are examples of the type first encountered on page 58.

p. 68: *Hikitara ba / kaku tsugu mono o /waga naka wa /*
nakanaka obi no / naka ni zo ara mashi

Naka appears four times in this poem; the pun is on the meanings "relationship" and "middle." (See the note to page 12.) *Nakanaka*, translated here a bit obliquely as "but," literally means "instead." The poem as a whole plays somewhat teasingly on the issue of what is torn, the belt or the relationship.

p. 69: *Akikaze no / oto ni tsukete mo / matare tsuru /*
koromo kasaneru / naka narane domo

"Overlapping clothes" was one of the usual ways of referring to sleeping together. The image is quite literal: lovers would use their many layers of kimonos as bedcovers.

p. 70: *Kakurenu mo / kai nakari keri / harukoma no /*
asare ba komo no / ne dani nokorazu

The original of this poem is not so clearly allegorical as the translation; in the original, the pond is not female, hence not so definitively an image for a court woman who has gone into the country for some (unobtained) respite from romantic intrigue. But this does seem the most likely reading of the poem.

p. 71: *Koe mo sen / kosazu mo aran / Ōsaka no /*
sekimori naranu / hito na togameso

Ōsaka is a pivot-word: an actual place name and also the mountain pass of "meeting." See the Introduction, page xxiv, for a further discussion of this poem.

p. 72: *Kotowari ni / ochishi namida wa / nagarete no /*
ukina o susugu / mizu to nara mashi

Literally, one who was the subject of gossip possessed a "floating name."

p. 73: *Kawaraji ya / take no hurune wa / hitoyo dani /*
kore ni tomareru / hushi wa ari ya to

As the headnote makes clear, recognized poets of high skill were at times solicited to compose poems on behalf of others. It is a fascinating insight into the role of poetry in the Heian court to think of a wife, now herself cheated on, seeking the sympathy of the prior wife she had wronged by means of a poem, let alone one written by someone else. Shikibu wrote cleverly for her friend: there are two sets of wordplay in this poem, involving the ideas of "root—sleeping together" and "node of bamboo—occasion—sleeping together."

p. 74: *Iwamashi o / ware ga tenare no / koma nara ba /*
hito ni shitagau / ayumi suna tomo

A prose headnote says that this poem was written after Shikibu saw her lover pass her gate on horseback. Once again, one can suppose that the horse of this poem is both real and allegorical.

p. 75: *Sono kata to / sashite mo yoranu / ukihune no /*
mata kogihanare / omou tomo nashi

p. 76: *Tadani shimo / hoshiai no sora / nagameji na /*
Ama no kawakaze / samuku huku nari

In Japan, the Milky Way is called Heaven's River.

Urayamashi / kyō o chigireru / tanabata ya /
itsu tomo shiranu / hito mo aru yo ni

p. 77: *Niwa no mama / yuruyuru ouru / natsukusa o /*
wakete bakari ni / kon hito mo gana

p. 78: *Niodori no / shita no kokoro wa / ika nare ya /*
minaruru mizu no / ue zo tsure naki

In the original of this poem, a pivot-word contributes more clearly the idea that the "grebe's" coolness may stem from his having grown too used to seeing the author.

p. 79: *Natsu no yo wa / maki no to tataki / kado tataki /*
hito tanome naru / kuina nari keri

Tataki—"knock" or "rap"—is wonderfully onomatopoetic in the original.

p. 80: *Hito shirenu / kokoro no uchi mo / mienu ran /*
ka bakari terasu / tsuki no hikari ni

This poem, like the one on page 73, was written on behalf of a friend, who, though shy, wished to invite a potential lover's interest.

p. 81: *Chiri no iru / mono to makura wa / narinu meri /*
nani no tame kawa / uchi mo harawan

p. 82: *Nugisuten / kata naki momo wa / karagoromo /*
tachi to tachi nuru / na ni koso ari keri

A "Chinese robe" symbolizes a bad reputation. *Tachi*, here repeated twice, means both "stood" and "cut"—thus, the pivot-word says that though Shikibu tried and tried to cut away the Chinese robe, she could not: it, and her floating—here translated as "gossip-muddied"—name continued to stand.

p. 83: *Izure o ka / yo ni nakare to wa / omou beki /*
wasururu hito to / wasuraruru mi to

Naki hito o / nakute koin to / ari nagara /
ai mizaran to / izure masareri

Omoe domo / yoso naru naka to / katsu mitsutsu /
omowanu naka to / izure masareri

Hayaki se to / mizu no nagare to / hito no yo to /
tomaranu koto wa / izure masareri

Heian poets commonly wrote poems in lists. Shikibu also wrote lists of "Sorrowful Things," "Things as I Wish They Would Be," and "Mysterious Things."

p. 84: *Eda goto ni / hana chirimagae / ima wa tote /*
haru no sugiyuku / michi mienu made

The first sentence of this poem is in the imperative in the original, as if the poet herself were commanding the spring flowers to fall.

p. 85: *Izure tomo / wakare zari keri / haru no yo wa /*
tsuki koso hana no / nioi nari kere

This poem is a pure statement of enlightened mind, echoing its content in its enactment. A simple description of a visual image (the pale, glowing flower looking the same as the moon) also functions as metaphor, or, as it might be put in Buddhist terminology, as a finger pointing at the moon. The poem says, at this level of its meaning, that the world of small and transient things and the world of Enlightenment are one—an idea which is a fundamental part of Buddhist teaching. As the Chinese practitioner Layman P'ang said, "Do you want to know my miraculous powers? Carrying water, chopping wood." There is a tradition, in Buddhist training, that one complete an experience of awakening by composing a verse embodying that experience; perhaps this poem was written on such an occasion.

p. 86: *Yo no naka wa / kureyuku haru no / sue nare ya /*
kinō wa hana no / sakari to ka mishi

p. 87: *Sono koto to / iitemo nakanu / mushi no ne mo /*
kikinashi ni koso / kanashi kari keri

p. 88: *Yūgure ni / nado monoomoi no / masaru ran /*
matsu hito no mata / aru mi tomo nashi

p. 89: *Nagusamen / koto zo kanashiki / sumizome no /*
sode niwa tsuki no / kage mo tomarade

p. 90: *Kimi o mata / kaku miteshi gana / hakanakute /*
kozo wa kienishi / yuki mo huru meri

p. 91: *Nakazora ni / hitori ariake no / tsuki o mite /*
nokoru kuma naku / mi o zo shiri nuru

This poem, like the one on page 85, is deeply Buddhist in feeling, this time expressing a sense of oneness between the poet and the moon. A prose headnote tells us that at the time she was leading a complex romantic life, but, at least for the duration of the poem's underlying experience, all such concerns drop away.

p. 92: *Izuchi tote / isogu naru ran / izuko nimo /*
koyoi wa onaji / tsuki o koso mime

p. 93: *Shio no ma ni / mienu monomono / ari keri to /*
ama no amata ni / miseji to zo omou

Shio no ma, "daytime," also means "between the tides." The translation of this poem is somewhat free.

p. 94: *Aki huke ba / Tokiwa no yama no / matsukaze mo /*
irozuku bakari / mi ni zo shimi keru

p. 95: *Dareka kite / miru beki mono to / waga yado no /*
yomogyū arashi / hukiharau ran

p. 96: *Kaoru ka o / yosouru yori wa / hototogisu /*
kika baya onaji / koe ya shitaru to

The "nightingale" is the *hototogisu*, a bird native to Japan, variously designated "nightingale," "mountain cuckoo," "warbler," or "thrush" in translation. This poem appears near the beginning of Izumi Shikibu's *Diary*, a third-person account of her relationship with Prince Atsumichi (see the Introduction, page xxiv). The description offered there of the making of this poem is a good illustration of the role poetry from the past played in the lives, feelings, and writings of members of the Heian court. Upon receiving the prince's gift, Shikibu immediately thought of an anonymous poem from the *Kokinshū*: "In the scent of these orange blossoms waiting for May, I find the long-vanished fragrance of his robes." She then composed her reply to his gift, which, in saying "Rather than recall / in these flowers / the fragrance," simultaneously demonstrates that she is familiar with the earlier poem and refers to her own previous relationship with Atsumichi's brother. She has done all this in a scant twelve syllables by using the content of the earlier poem as part of the meaning of hers, so she still has time to invite the prince to send a poem of his own. In this translation we have attempted to resolve the problem of ignorance of the earlier work somewhat by adding the phrase *of the past* to *fragrance*.

p. 97: *Yo no tsune no / koto tomo sara ni / omooezu /*
hajimete mono o / omou ashita wa

This and many, though not all, of the next group of poems also come from the time of Shikibu's relationship with Prince Atsumichi.

p. 98: *Tō o koyo / saku to miru ma ni / chirinu beshi /*
tsuyu to hana to no / naka zo yo no naka

p. 99: *Matsu wa sono / moto no iro dani / aru mono o /*
subete midori mo / haru wa kotonari

It is interesting to compare this poem with the one by Komachi on page 17, to see how the same idea (that evergreens do not change color with the seasons) can be used as the basis of poems widely different in meaning.

p. 100: *Au koto o / iki no o ni suru / mi ni shi are ba / tayuru mo ikaga / kanashi to omowanu*

p. 101: *Kinō made / nani nageki ken / kesa no ma ni / koi koso wa ito / kurushi kari kere*

p. 102: *Mie mo sen / mi mo sen hito o / asa goto ni / okitewa mukau / kagami tomo gana*

p. 103: *Haru no yo wa / i koso nerare ne / okii tsutsu / mamoru ni tomaru / mono naranakuni*

p. 104: *Kokoromi ni / ame mo hura nan / kado sugite / sora iku tsuki no / kage ya tomaru to*

p. 105: *Waga kokoro / natsu no nobe nimo / aranaku ni / shigeku mo koi no / narimasaru kana*

p. 106: *Kuina dani / tataku oto se ba / maki no to o / kokoroyori nimo / akete mite mashi*

p. 107: *Yūgure wa / ikanaru toki zo / me ni mienu / kaze no oto sae / aware narukana*

p. 108: *Yoso nite mo / onaji kokoro ni / ariake no / tsuki mi ba sora zo / kakikumora mashi*

p. 109: *Yomosugara / nanigoto o kawa / omoi tsuru / mado utsu ame no / oto o kiki tsutsu*

This poem comes from the *Diary*, so we not only know the circumstances which prompted it but also have the poem Prince Atsumichi wrote in reply. Shikibu's poem, responding to a note from the prince asking how she had passed the previous stormy night, is clearly a reproach for the fact that she spent the night alone. The prince's answer is solicitous, depending on a pivot-word meaning both "husband" and "sheltering caves": "I also spent the long night pondering, thinking how the house without a husband has no solid caves."

p. 110: *Shinonome ni / okite wakareshi / hito yori wa /*
hisashiku tomaru / take no ha no tsuyu

This poem, inscribed on a fan that pictured a dewdrop on a leaf of bamboo, refers of course to the early-morning departures of Shikibu's lover.

p. 111: *Ajiki naku / haru wa inochi no / oshiki kana /*
hana zo ko no yo no / hodashi nari keru

This poem is fundamentally Buddhist in concept, with its reminder that attachment to the beauty of things of the world, even to life itself, is only a source of pain.

p. 112: *Kimi kouru / kokoro wa chiji ni / kudakere do /*
hitotsu mo usenu / mono ni zo ari keru

p. 113: *Orite mishi / hito no nioi ni / omooete /*
tsune yori oshiki / haru no hana kana

p. 114: *Isaya mata / kawaru mo shirazu / ima koso wa /*
hito no kokoro o / mite mo narawame

p. 115: *Nakanaka ni / ukarishi mama ni / yami ni se ba / wasururu hodo ni / nari mo shina mashi*

p. 116: *Huyu no hi o / mijikaki mono to / ii nagara / akuru ma dani mo / shiguru naru kana*

p. 117: *Hana mo mina / yo hukuru kaze ni / chirinu ran / nani o ka asu no / nagusame ni sen*

p. 118: *Sayonaka ni / tsuki o mi tsutsu mo / taga sato ni / yukitomarite mo / nagamu ran to wa*

It may be worth noticing that the word for midnight, *sayonaka*, contains the word *naka*, relationship.

p. 119: *Nakanaka ni / hagi no ha o dani / musubise ba / kaze niwa tokuru / oto mo shite mashi*

Lovers did tie written vows to leaves of bush clover.

p. 120: *Namidagawa / onaji mi yori wa / nagarure do / koi o ba ketanu / mono ni zo ari keru*

p. 121: *Neya no ue ni / shimo ya oku ran / kata shikeru / shita koso itaku / saenoboru nare*

p. 122: *Kono yo niwa / ikaga sadamen / onozu kara / mukashi o towan / hito ni toe kashi*

p. 123: *Satobito no / koromo utsu naru / tsuchi no ne ni / ayanaku ware mo / nezamenuru kana*

Fulling cloth is an activity traditionally associated with autumn. It was not uncommon for members of the court to go to the countryside, sometimes on their own for a retreat, other times in the company of their lovers—these meetings needed to be arranged with great discretion.

p. 124: *Ato o mite / shinobu mo ayashi / yume nite mo /*
nanigoto no mata / arishi to mo naku

p. 125: *Toshi o hete / mono omou koto wa / narai ni ki /*
hana ni wakarenu / haru shi nakere ba

Tanomu tote / tanomi keru koso / hakana kere /
hiruma no yume no / yo towa shirazu ya

p. 126: *Kaku bakari / kaze wa huke domo / ita no ma mo /*
awane ba tsuki no / kage sae zo moru

This poem's power and resonance emerge when one reads it as a Buddhist statement: it is in the midst of poverty and suffering that the moonlight of enlightenment is able to enter the human heart. A more literal translation of the poem is "Although the wind blows hard [literally, like this], the moon's light also leaks in when the wooden planks don't meet."

p. 127: *Itazura ni / mi o zo sutetsuru / hito omou /*
kokoro ya hukaki / tani to naru ran

p. 128: *Wabinure ba / kemuri o dani mo / taeji tote /*
shiba ori takeru / huyu no yamazato

p. 129: *Omowaji o / aretaru yado ni / kakikurasu /*
kumo no igaki ni / kaze shi tamara ba

p. 130: *Nishi e yuku / kumo ni norinan to / omou mi no /*
kokoro bakari wa / kita e yuku kana

p. 131: *Yume ni dani / mie mo ya suru to / shikitae no /*
makura ugokite / i dani nerarezu

p. 132: *Mizu kōru / huyu dani kure ba / ukikusa no /*
ono ga kokoro to / nezasbigao naru

Literally, the floating grass puts on a "root face." The rhetorical strategy of this poem is very different from that of most of Shikibu's work. The poem on page 126 (see its note for a fairly literal translation) is somewhat similar in that it also devotes itself to a description seemingly outside the poet's subjective experience; yet in that case it is easy to imagine the poet writing from inside the situation of the poem. Here the work of the poem takes place wholly within what T. S. Eliot called the "objective correlative"—the external image which becomes the perfect embodiment of a particular experience. The meaning of the poem is obliquely hortatory: when painful but inevitable circumstances arrive, one should be like those floating reeds, which pretend that their winter immobility is something they chose.

p. 133: *Ume wa baya / saki ni keri tote / ore ba chiru /*
hana to zo yuki no / huru wa mie kere

Another interpretation of this poem is also possible: "This falling snow, so much like falling flowers—if someone cut a branch, he'd say, 'The plum has already bloomed.'"

p. 134: *Matsu hito no / ima mo kitara ba / ikaga sen /*
humamaku oshiki / niwa no yuki kana

Shikibu has waited through the night, once again, for a lover who did not appear—this time, however, she has transcended the situation. This poem is slightly reminiscent of Wallace Stevens's "The Snow Man":

> One must have a mind of winter
> To regard the frost and the boughs
> Of the pine-trees crusted with snow . . .
>
> and not to think
> Of any misery in the sound of the wind . . .

Shikibu has achieved this "mind of winter," accepting both what is there and what is not, at one with things as they are.

p. 135: *Au koto ni / yorozu masaranu / mono nara ba /*
ii niwa iwa de / omoi ni zo omou

p. 136: *Aki huku wa / ikanaru iro no / kaze nare ba /*
mi ni shimu bakari / aware naru ran

p. 137: *Tokotowa ni / aware aware wa / tsukusu to mo /*
kokoro ni kanau / mono ka inochi wa

This poem was written in response to a man's request to think of him sometimes with love in the future.

p. 138: *Ukinagara / nagarau kata ni / aru mono o /*
nanika ko no yo ni / shū mo todomen

In the Heian era, books were duplicated only by hand copying. *Shū* is a pivot-word, meaning both "collection" and "attachment" or "clinging," in its Buddhist sense. The fact that this poem of nonattachment to the written word was written by the author of over a thousand poems makes it especially moving. The underlying idea that everything is subject to change and that, as a result, the attempt to cling to anything is a source of suffering is also reflected in the poem on page 111.

p. 139: *Chikaku miru / hito mo wagami mo / katagata ni /*
tadayou kumo to / naran to su ran

p. 140: *Hana yori mo / ne zo mimahoshiki / ominaeshi /*
ōkaru nobe o / horimotome tsutsu

p. 141: *Kokoro niwa / hitotsu minori to / omoe domo /*
mushi wa koegoe / kikoyu naru kana

It is hard to tell from this poem if Shikibu is truly troubled by hearing the crickets (the voice of the world beyond the temple), or, for that matter, if we ought even to think that she should be. The name of one of the main figures in Buddhism, Avalokitesvara (known in Japan as Kwannon), translates as "The One Who Hears the Cries of the World."

p. 142: *Mono o nomi / omoi no ie o / idete huru /*
ichimi no ame ni / nure ya shina mashi

This poem contains three references to the Lotus Sutra, whose central message is that although Buddhist teaching can take many forms, according to time and circumstance, there is ultimately only one Way. Each of the references is to an illustration of this idea. In the first, *omoi* is used as a pivot-word, with the dual meanings of "thinking" and "burning." The burning house as an image for the world of delusion comes from a story intended to illustrate the concept of skillful means: A father sees his children playing inside a house they do not realize is on fire; because they refuse at first to come when he calls them, he describes three fascinating toys (representing the three main schools of Buddhist teaching) he has with him in the yard. But when the children, enticed by his description, run out, they see that in fact what awaits them is only a single cart drawn by a white bull: the Buddha's one teaching. The second and third references, translated here as "taste the pure rain's / single truth," are in the phrase *ichimi no ame*, which means literally "the one taste rain." The image-concept underlying "one taste" is this: just as the ocean appears in many forms and places but is everywhere suffused with the single flavor of salt, the teaching has only one flavor. The rain comes from a description in the sutra's fifth chapter of the way one rain falling from the sky nourishes many kinds of plants and beings.

p. 143: *O o yowami / taete midaruru / tama yori mo /*
nukitomegatashi / hito no inochi wa

This poem is one of a series written in the form of an acrostic—the sentence spelled out in the acrostic, from the *Hokke Kyo Kanjibon*, is "I keep back neither body nor life."

p. 144: *Hure ba yo no / itodo uki mi no / shiraruru o /*
kyō nagaame ni / mizu masaru ran

p. 145: *Yama o idete / kuraki michi ni o / tazunekoshi /*
ima hitotabi no / au koto ni yori

p. 146: *Yūgure wa / kimi ga kayoiji / michi mo naku /*
sugakeru kumo no / ito zo kanashiki

When Prince Atsumichi died, Shikibu wrote 249 poems of mourning. The poems here are selected from this group, although poems from this period also appear elsewhere in this book.

Keburi nan / koto zo kanashiki / utsusemi no /
munashiki kara mo / ara ba koso are

The smoke in this poem is a literal reference to cremation.

p. 147: *Mono omoe ba / sawa no hotaru mo / wagami yori /*
akugareizuru / tama ka to zo miru

Another, virtually literal, translation: "While thinking things [of her dead lover], the marsh's fireflies seem like the soul's jewels and longings wandering out of my body." "Thinking things" is a standard phrase for remembering. "Soul's jewels," is the usual phrase for referring to the substance of one's spirit; because this meaning would not be recognized by Western readers, we have used the somewhat more familiar image of the "spark" of life.

Nagusamete / hikari no ma nimo / arubeki o /
mietewa mienu / yoi no inazuma

p. 148: *Hakanakute / keburi to narishi / hito ni yori /*
kumoi no sora no / mutsumajiki kana

Again, the smoke is a literal reference to cremation.

Onogajishi / hi dani kurure ba / tobu tori no /
izukata ni kawa / kimi o tazunen

p. 149: *Tamasudare / tarekomete nomi / neshi toki wa /*
akuchō koto mo / shirare ya wa seshi

Yo ni huredo / kimi ni okurete / oru hana wa /
nioite miezu / sumizome ni shite

p. 150: *Kataraishi / koe zo koishiki / omokage wa /*
arishi so nagara / mono mo iwane ba

Naki hito no / kuru yo to kikedo / kimi mo nashi /
waga sumu sato ya / tama naki no sato

p. 151: *Sutehaten to / omou sae koso / kanashi kere /*
kimi ni narenishi / wagami to omoe ba

Tomokaku mo / iwa ba nabete ni / narinu beshi /
ne ni koso nakite / misemahoshi kere

p. 152: *Morotomo ni / ikade hiruma ni / narinure do /*
sasuga ni shinan / mi o ika ni sen

Sayaka ni mo / hito wa miru ran / waga me niwa /
namida ni kumoru / yoi no tsukikage

p. 153: *Inochi ara ba / ikasama ni sen / yo o shiranu /*
mushi dani aki wa / naki ni koso nake

Akazarishi / mukashi no koto o / kakitsukuru /
suzuri no mizu wa / namida nari keri

p. 154: *Yami ni nomi / madou mi nare ba / sumizome no /*
sode wa hiru to mo / shirare zari keri

Hiru is a pivot-word meaning both "dry" and "daytime." Thus, there is no time when her sleeves are dry [when she does not weep] and no time when she is able to know day.

p. 155 *Nadote kimi / munashiki sora ni / kie ni ken /*
awayuki dani mo / hure ba huru yo ni

Vanishing into empty sky is, like the smoke of the poems on pages 146 and 148, a literal reference to cremation.

Koiwabu to / kiki ni dani kike / kane no ne ni /
uchiwasuraruru / toki no ma zo naki

The large bells in Japanese temples are struck, then allowed to resonate; the next hit comes just before the last one subsides into silence.

p. 156: *Kagiri are ba / huji no koromo wa / nugisutete /*
namida no iro o / somete koso kire

p. 157: *Ukiyo o ba / itoi nagara mo / ika de ka wa /*
kono yo no koto o / omoisutsu beki

p. 158: *Hototogisu / katarai okite / shide no yama /*
koe ba kono yo no / shiru hito ni sen

A prose headnote says that this poem was written when Shikibu was lying in bed ill and heard the calling of a *hototogisu*, or mountain cuckoo, the bird that is traditionally believed to accompany the soul into death.

p. 159: *Kuraki yori / kuraki michi ni zo / irinu beki /*
haruka ni terase / yama no ha no tsuki

The tradition that this poem was written on Shikibu's deathbed comes from a prose headnote which indicates that it was "Sent to His Eminence, Priest Shoku" and is further strengthened by the phrase "through darkness to darkness," which refers to a passage from the Lotus Sutra: "The long night further curses our fate: we pass into darkness from darkness." *Michi*, "way," is the word commonly chosen for a literal path, but it has the dual meaning of Buddhist practice, the Way; mountains, we know from the previous poem, can be a symbol for death. The mountains, the path, the moon all work to present an image entirely true to the physical world; by combining this literally sound imagery and the evocative connotations of each carefully chosen word and phrase, the poem becomes a deeply moving call: as she moves from the darkness and confusion of human life and suffering towards the darkness of the unknowable future, Shikibu asks for the clarifying moon of enlightenment to remain with her for a few moments longer before disappearing.

If the legend that this was her final poem is true, the last word Shikibu wrote was "moon."

VINTAGE CLASSICS

Vintage launched in the United Kingdom in 1990, and was originally the paperback home for the Random House Group's literary authors. Now, Vintage comprises some of London's oldest and most prestigious literary houses, including Chatto & Windus (1855), Hogarth (1917), Jonathan Cape (1921) and Secker & Warburg (1935), alongside the newer or relaunched hardback and paperback imprints: The Bodley Head, Harvill Secker, Yellow Jersey, Square Peg, Vintage Paperbacks and Vintage Classics.

From Angela Carter, Graham Greene and Aldous Huxley to Toni Morrison, Haruki Murakami and Virginia Woolf, Vintage Classics is renowned for publishing some of the greatest writers and thinkers from around the world and across the ages – all complemented by our beautiful, stylish approach to design. Vintage Classics' authors have won many of the world's most revered literary prizes, including the Nobel, the Booker, the Prix Goncourt and the Pulitzer, and through their writing they continue to capture imaginations, inspire new perspectives and incite curiosity.

In 2007 Vintage Classics introduced its distinctive red spine design, and in 2012 Vintage Children's Classics was launched to include the much-loved authors of our childhood. Random House joined forces with the Penguin Group in 2013 to become Penguin Random House, making it the largest trade publisher in the United Kingdom.

@vintagebooks

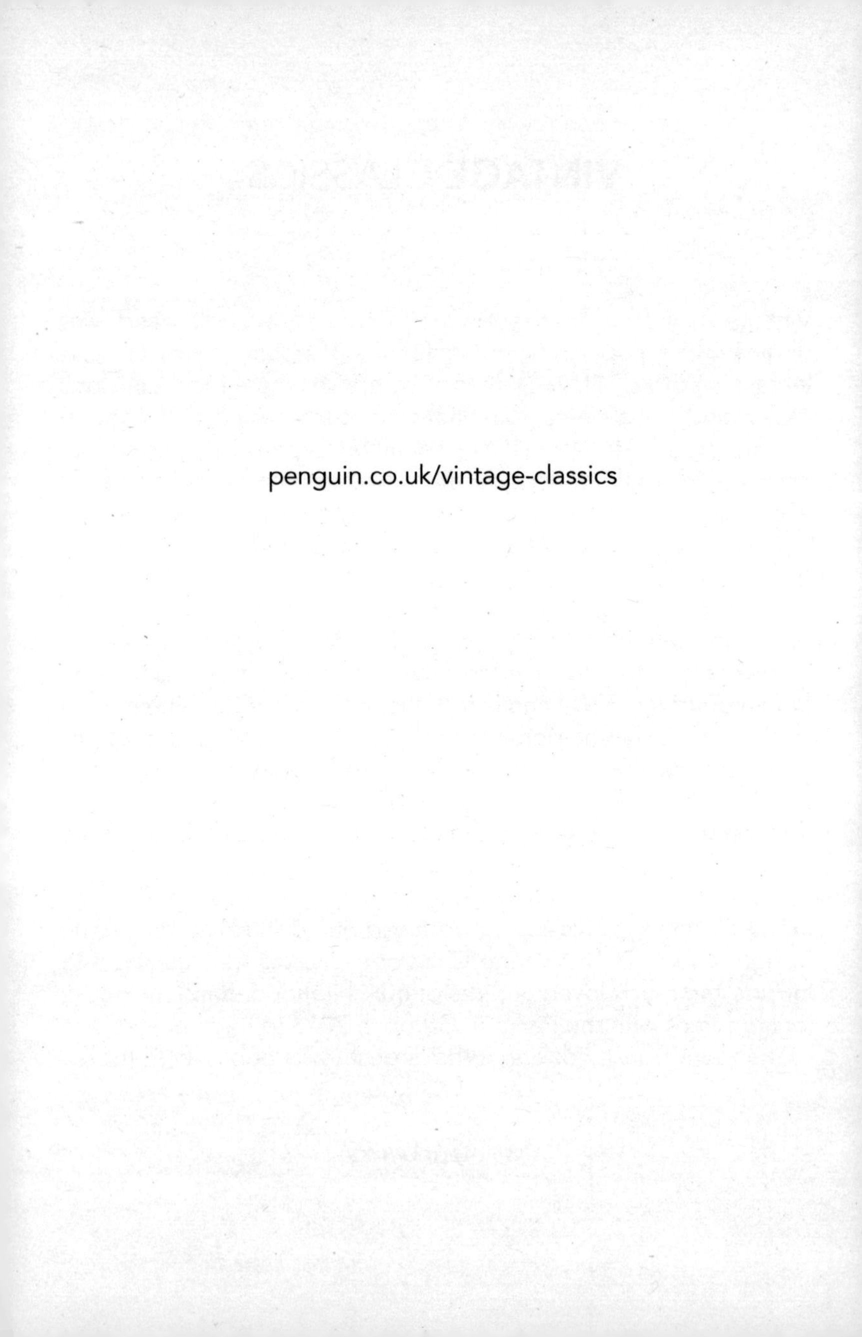

penguin.co.uk/vintage-classics